D0927382

LIVING
THE LECTIONARY

LIVING
THE LECTIONARY
LINKS TO LIFE AND LITERATURE

YEAR B

GEOFF WOOD

LITURGY
TRAINING
PUBLICATIONS

Acknowledgments

We are grateful to the many publishers and authors who have given permission to include their work. Every effort has been made to determine the ownership of all texts and to make proper arrangement for their use. We will gladly correct in future editions any oversight or error that is brought to our attention.

Excerpt from *Altogether Different Language,* by Anne Porter, published by Zoland Books, an imprint of Steerforth Press of Hanover, New Hampshire. Copyright © 1994 Anne Porter.

Excerpt from "For the Time Being," copyright 1944 and renewed 1972 by W. H. Auden, from *Collected Poems* by W. H. Auden. Used by permission of Random House, Inc.

Excerpts from "A Visit of Charity" and "A Worn Path" in A *Curtain of Green and Other Stories,* copyright 1941 and renewed 1969 by Eudora Welty, reprinted by permission of Harcourt, Inc.

Excerpt from *The Giver* by Lois Lowry. Copyright © 1999 by Lois Lowry. Reproduced by permission of Houghton Mifflin Company. All rights reserved.

Acknowledgments continued on page 162.

LIVING THE LECTIONARY: LINKS TO LIFE AND LITERATURE, YEAR B © 2005 Archdiocese of Chicago: Liturgy Training Publications, 1800 North Hermitage Avenue, Chicago IL 60622-1101; 1-800-933-1800, fax 1-800-933-7094, e-mail orders@ltp.org. All rights reserved. See our website at www.ltp.org.

This book was edited by Kris Fankhouser. The design is by Anna Manhart, and the typesetting was done by Kari Nicholls in Minion.

Printed in the United States of America.

Library of Congress Control Number: 2005927972

ISBN 1-56854-527-4

LIVLB

Contents

FIRST SUNDAY OF ADVENT

Isaiah 63:16b–17, 19b; 64:2b–7, Mark 13:33–37, Betty Smith

Oh, That You Would Rend the Heavens

Very often, when problems escalate and there seems to be no relief in sight, even nonbelievers resort to prayer (if only reflexively), demanding of God or "somebody" to intervene, to change night into day. Believers do no less, as when my teenage son seemed inextricably addicted to drugs, so that I found myself one day literally driving my fist into a wall, crying out to God, "Do something! Prove you exist! Save my son!"

The prophet in today's first reading must have shared the same frustration, if on a larger scale. For he was witness to a catastrophe of national scope, the destruction of his homeland and its temple and the exile of his people to Babylon. And so he calls on God to pull off another Exodus, to intervene in the spectacular way he did 700 years earlier when he opened the Red Sea, fed his people manna in the desert, quenched their thirst with water from a rock, and finally became explosively present on the summit of Mount Sinai as a guarantee of his existence and support.

"Oh, that you would rend the heavens and come down," he cries, "with the mountains quaking before you, while you wrought awesome deeds we could not hope for." And so it seems that the greater our frustration over whatever oppresses us, the more vehement our cry for help, the less we're inclined to settle for anything but a miracle.

But does God ever intervene in spectacular ways? It's true; his past interventions are often recorded as spectacular. But how much of that is the product of later poetic embellishment even as the brief skirmish at Lexington in 1775 is now remembered as the *Battle* of Lexington because of its then unforeseen consequences? And—on his trek back to the Sinai of Moses—did not the forlorn prophet Elijah discover God to be present not in any cyclone or earthquake or thunder and lightning (as he might have hoped) but in what the scriptures describe as "a still small voice," a gentle breeze?

That's the way God seems to make his presence felt in Betty Smith's *A Tree Grows in Brooklyn*. We're back in early twentieth-century New York where the widowed Katie Nolan and her children, Francie and Neeley, lived amid the poverty-ridden tenements of Brooklyn's Williamsburg neighborhood. Indeed, making ends meet had been so difficult that Katie learned early to live without illusions. She became a hard-nosed realist and taught her kids to steer clear of the romantic expectations of their now deceased father, who lived in a world of "Sweet Rosie O'Grady" and other sentimental ballads.

Yet throughout the story, epiphanies of God do happen, if ever so gently, as when, to celebrate Francie's graduation from elementary school, Katie took her and Neeley and their two aunts to an ice cream parlor for a rare treat. Eventually the waiter placed down the check for 30 cents. Aunt Evy hoped impoverished Katie would feel justified in not leaving a tip. Neely, on the other hand, would have felt embarrassed if she didn't leave a nickel. Katie had only a 50-cent coin in her purse, so she laid it on the check. The waiter returned with four nickels and thought how much bread that meant to her family. Everyone watched. Then without further hesitation Katie left the four nickels on the table, grandly telling the waiter to keep the change. Francie wanted to stand up and cheer!

And then there was that midnight gesture on New Year's Eve, 1917. Francie had thrown open the window of their top floor flat. The author describes the city as very still until a church bell began to toll, followed by other bells. Then came whistles, a siren, and the tinny noise of horns. Then someone began "Auld Lang Syne" and the Irish joined in, but only to be outdone by the neighborhood Germans singing, *"Ja, das ist ein Gartenhaus."* Soon there were cat-calls. The moment degenerated into insults. The Jews and Italians withdrew behind their blinds, leaving the fight to the Germans and the Irish. Finally all settled down; once more the night was quiet.

And then and only then did Francie, her mother, and Neeley stand together before their open window and shout out into the silence, "Happy New Year, everybody!"

Surely God arrives among us at such moments! Spectacularly? No. But ever so truly nevertheless. He's present in the spontaneous generosity of Katie, in the imaginative initiative of Francie, relieving the bleakness of tenement existence, offering proof that goodness exists, that God exists as a graciousness, a magnanimity latent within our breasts that, if released even in the simplest ways, can transfigure a neighborhood, transfigure a world—as, for example, whenever you and I might have the guts someday—like Katie—to leave somebody a 66 percent tip!

And so how might God ultimately respond to the prayer of the frustrated prophet of our first reading? By way of an exploding mountain or in ways ear has not heard, nor eye ever seen? Not likely. He will intervene in a way less obvious, as someone who has arrived too late to find a room in a village inn. He will arrive as a newborn infant in a manger—a mere census statistic as far as the world is concerned. In other words, he will arrive as unspectacularly as you and I, which we might take as a signal that God might even reveal himself in unspectacular you and me, if in some way we have learned to breathe the very Spirit that within the next few weeks will bring Christ so quietly yet so wonderfully into our world.

SECOND SUNDAY OF ADVENT

Isaiah 40:1–5,9–11, William Blake

Fourfold Vision

In an 1802 letter to Thomas Butts, the mystical poet William Blake wrote verses that include the following:

> Now I fourfold vision see,
> And a fourfold vision is given to me;
> 'Tis fourfold in my supreme delight
> And threefold in soft Beulah's night
> And twofold Always. May God us keep
> From Single vision & Newton's sleep![1]

So, according to Blake, we human beings are capable of four kinds of vision, namely:

> *Fourfold:* Here I see the unity of all things; you and I and nature are one; here I see and behave creatively in the manner of God the Creator; I see and create beauty and good; I see energetically; my eyes and all my senses are driven by faith, hope, and love.

> *Threefold:* Here I see with affection and warmth; I see you and I sense "thou."

> *Twofold:* Here I see things and people as mere facts, the inanimate furniture of my environment; I sense no connection; I behold all from a distance, aloof.

> *Single:* Here I see no one but myself, my opinion, the world according "me."

Along with Adam and Eve, we were made to enjoy threefold and fourfold vision, to view reality through eyes of love, to be co-creators of a Paradise with God. But somehow we slipped into a state of twofold and single vision. We now live disconnected, within a cosmic cocoon fashioned by our fear and resentments, individually and as societies. Or to put it another way, we have fallen into what amounts to a deep sleep of twofold and single vision, a state of indifference, loneliness, suspicion, and the nightmares they generate.

Realizing this, we cry out by way of last Sunday's Advent scripture readings to be liberated. We cry out for Christ to come from the realm of fourfold and threefold vision to awaken us, to open our eyes and hearts once more to view things the way he sees them and behave as he behaves. Isaiah gives voice to our cry: "O that you would tear open the heavens, this cocoon we have woven round ourselves. O that you would open our senses to perceive things awesome and unexpected the way your visionaries Moses and Abraham once did. We fade like leaves of autumn. No one calls upon your name; no one trusts that God and angels are really out there beyond the merely 'factual' world we've become so used to."

And today Isaiah intensifies his pleas: "Comfort your people, O God; speak tenderly to us, lost as we are in the fog of twofold and single vision. We've suffered long enough in this wilderness of mute 'nature' and self-interest."

And sure enough! Isaiah's pleading gets a response. A voice cries out: "Lay a road from the realm of fourfold and threefold vision straight into this wilderness of mere twofold and single vision— a road by which the splendor of God's world may enter—that they who walk in darkness may by way of revived faith begin to see dimensions of reality they never dared dream of. Say to the cities of myopic men: Here is your God. See, he comes to lead us back to that pastoral world, the garden world we've lost touch with—where affection and caring are supreme, where we shall find ourselves gathered up like lambs in the familiar arms of a Shepherd, instead of struggling to survive amid a world of strangers."

For mystics like Blake and the prophets, paradise was not a place remote in time and space. It's all around us, just the other side of the limits of single and twofold vision. All we need is love and genuine faith to have it begin to appear in all its wonder—as it did for the three disciples on Mount Tabor. Were I to let such love overcome my timidity, I would see everyone in this congregation transfigured—your worth and apparent and potential beauty resplendent—so much so that I might want to close my eyes, shield them. But why would I want to do that? Graduation to threefold and fourfold vision is our destiny and ultimate Yuletide gift.

THIRD SUNDAY OF ADVENT

Isaiah 61:1–2a, 10–11; John 1:6–8, 19–28, Marcel Proust

Bethlehem 'round the Bend

It was with much anxiety that the adolescent Marcel (in Proust's novel *In Search of Lost Time)* boarded a train in Paris and set off on his first journey to the seaside resort of Balbec. He was a boy who depended on a familiar environment and predictable routine to feel secure and this excursion to a strange location threatened to trigger one of his asthma attacks. Nevertheless, Marcel spent a peaceful night in his compartment and awoke to see the sunrise through the pale square of his window.

Slowly the train came to a temporary stop at a little station between two mountains and Marcel caught sight of a tall girl emerging from a house and climbing a path bathed by the slanting rays of the sun. She was approaching the station carrying a jar of milk.

> In her valley from which the rest of the world was hidden by
> these heights, she must never see anyone save in these trains
> which stopped for a moment only. She passed down the line

of windows, offering coffee and milk to a few awakened
passengers. Flushed with the glow of morning, her face
was rosier than the sky.[2]

Marcel goes on to recall that he "felt in seeing her that desire
to live which is reborn in us whenever we become conscious anew of
beauty and happiness." Normally his routine way of life would have
insulated him from noticing anything or anyone beautiful, but here
at a remote train stop situated in a strange landscape his insulation
had given way. He was open to the impact of this apparition. He was
ready to get off the train of habit and spend the rest of his life with
this lovely apparition. He signaled her to bring him some coffee.

She did not see me; I called to her . . . . She retraced her steps.
I could not take my eyes from her face which grew larger as
she approached, like a sun . . . dazzling you with its blaze
of red and gold. She fastened on me her penetrating gaze,
but doors were being closed and the train had begun to move.
I saw her leave the station and go down the hill to her home;
it was broad daylight now; I was speeding away from the dawn.

I can't help but think of Marcel's train as an image descrip-
tive of my life and perhaps yours. Doesn't life for all of us become in
some way a narrow corridor of habit—set on wheels that convey us
rapidly through time, equipped, yes, with windows through which
we can catch a glimpse of the passing years, a passing landscape—
of other people and an occasional sunrise? Otherwise our consciousness is confined—like that of the captives in Isaiah's first reading
and the Levites of today's Gospel—to the familiar enclosure in
which we are lulled to sleep by the "clickety clack" of those wheels
that relentlessly carry us through one day after another.

Until, thank God, we slow down enough to arrive at a
station called Christmas, where we have at least a chance to stick
our heads out the window and see the Virgin Mary "flushed with

the glow of morning," offering us, if not a pitcher of milk, then a nourishment even more profound: her newborn son who is destined one day to become our eucharistic bread and wine!

But do we allow ourselves to savor this season of spiritual sunrise? Do we stay long enough in Bethlehem to allow Christmas to do for us what Marcel's experience of that milkmaid did for him? How does he describe it?

> It gave a tonality to all I saw, introduced me as an actor upon the stage of an unknown and infinitely more interesting universe . . . from which to emerge now would be, as it were, to die to myself.

Time to sit up now! The narrow coach of habit that so confines your limbs and vision and mind and soul is coming 'round the bend. Bethlehem lies just ahead, offering you the vision of a real sunrise and of a lovely lady dressed in blue and the experience—if only for a moment—of a world permeated with the poetry of God's Word made flesh.

FOURTH SUNDAY OF ADVENT

2 Samuel 7:1–5, 8b–12, 14a, 16

Pastorale

One could say that Christmas is all about Abel's getting even with Cain. The Bible begins with the story of Cain, the sodbuster and builder of the first city, killing Abel, the peaceable shepherd. It is a story that reflects Israel's sympathy for Abel and its lasting nostalgia for a pastoral versus Cain's city way of life—much the way a Cheyenne American living in a cramped apartment in Los Angeles might dream of the wandering ways of his forefathers.

Abraham, the father of Israel, was a nomad, a keeper of sheep and goats. He wandered about the high country above the turmoil of the Canaanite cities below. Lot, his nephew, let himself be seduced by urban life and forsook shepherding to live in rapacious Sodom, and we know what happened to him! Isaac, too, was a shepherd. So were Jacob and his sons. Moses, who grew up in the imperial cities of Egypt, underwent a spiritual breakthrough only after he left Egypt and went shepherding on the wide-open range of Sinai. And so it was that Israel never quite forgot its nomadic origins even after the nation settled down, took up farming, and become urbanized like the nations around her.

Israel's holy men became concerned about this drift away from green pastures to walled-in city living with its kings, bureaucracies, and potential for economic inequity. So they insisted that if the Israelite tribes must unite into a kingdom under a monarch, that monarch should be a shepherd. They wanted kings strongly rooted in the nation's pastoral origins. That's why the shepherd Saul and eventually that Bethlehem shepherd David were chosen to be their first royal leaders.

But was it only nostalgia that made them do this? No, it went deeper than that. Shepherding was symbolic of freedom, mobility, flexibility, a hankering after wide-open spaces and starry skies where one felt closer to God. It also said something about gentleness, concern for things vulnerable, a willingness to protect the weak and confront the ravenous elements of this universe. These were qualities worth remembering and maintaining, especially when the pressures of urban life and royal politics might tempt Israel to become like so many other nations: hard, polarized, aggressive, even lethal like Cain. It's no wonder then that when Israel's initial experiment in monarchy failed, when so many of its kings lost touch with the simpler things of life and became tyrants, its prophets looked with longing to Bethlehem from which, perhaps, a more benevolent and pastoral king like David might come to get Israel moving and capable of being moved once more in the spiritual and just sense of the word.

We believe this Shepherd King has come. His arrival was not noticed in the urban centers of Caesar's empire, except as a digit recorded by Caesar's census takers. No, this ultimate Shepherd King was initially recognized only by other shepherds, as might be expected. But ever since, he has come to be known throughout the world as the Good Shepherd and, as such, has revealed to us in the flesh the true nature of this world's Creator—which is not at all cantankerous like that of the harried princes of Cain's citadels but has been best described in that most beautiful of psalms:

> The Lord is my Shepherd, I shall not want.
> He maketh me to lie down in green pastures:
> he leadeth me beside still waters;
> He restoreth my soul: he leadeth me in the
> paths of righteousness for his name's sake.
> Yea, though I walk through the valley of the shadow of death,
> I will fear no evil: for thou art with me;
> thy rod and thy staff they comfort me.[3]

THE NATIVITY OF THE LORD
MASS DURING THE DAY

Isaiah 52:7–10, Betty Smith

How Beautiful upon the Mountains

I remember how I used to accompany my father on Christmas Eve as he ventured forth at around 10:00 or 11:00 PM to find street corners where Christmas trees that hadn't been sold were being given away. It embarrassed me a bit because it signaled to the people passing by that our family was too strapped for income to afford one. But then so was almost every family we knew, it being the decade of the Great Depression—the 1930s. This is why I can so readily identify with the Christmas experience of Francie and Neeley Nolan in Betty Smith's *A Tree Grows in Brooklyn*. (I draw from this story in the course of these essays to show how one novel can be mined for so many fresh parables to enhance the message of our biblical heritage.)

Francie and Neeley, a few decades before my own childhood, were wandering through the streets of their neighborhood at midnight of Christmas Eve looking for a free evergreen. The way it worked at that late hour was that the tree salesman made a contest of it. He took each unsold tree and challenged any kid to catch it without falling down under its breadth and weight. If you stayed on your feet, the tree was yours. Now that worked well for the bigger boys, but Francie was only ten and her brother nine, and the tree Francie chose to contend for was ten feet high. The salesman agreed to let her brother help her.

Indeed, he felt some remorse in making them go through this somewhat sadistic game, but then he thought these kids needed to face up to the harsh realities of life. They had to learn to compete for what they wanted. So much for the Christmas spirit! Anyway, he heaved the ample tree toward the children, causing them to stagger blindly amid its green and prickly branches. But Francie and Neeley kept their feet and won their precious prize.

When they somewhat awkwardly reached the door of their tenement, their father came down to help them carry it up the stairwell to their top floor flat, while Papa sang "Holy Night" all the way. Papa pulled from above and the children pushed from below. "The narrow walls took up his clear sweet voice . . . and gave it back with doubled sweetness. Doors creaked open and families gathered on the landings, pleased and amazed at the something unexpected being added to that moment of their lives." The spinster Tynmore sisters, "their gray hair in crimpers," stood in their doorway and began to sing. The flirtatious Flossie Gaddis, her mother, and her brother (who was slowly dying of consumption) looked out. As Floss leaned seductively against the doorjamb, causing Francie's father to suggest that for want of an angel to top off the tree, perhaps Flossie might serve the purpose.

Finally, they set up the tree in their small front room. Its branches spread out to fill the space, draped over the piano and chairs. They couldn't afford to decorate it. But the tree was orna-ment enough—a grand, aromatic intrusion of mystery confined within the perimeter of a tin bucket. And oh the mystery of this world's Creator, the Root of Jesse, the Ground of all Being, resting in a manger among us, come to make our whole world aromatic with divine grace!

But what impresses me most about this episode is how the ascent of that Christmas tree, symbolic of Eden's Tree of Life and the redemptive cross of Christ and of Christ the true Vine of which we are his branches—what impresses me most is how it brought the flat dwellers out of their closed apartments to assemble on the various levels of that ascending staircase (symbolic of Jacob's ladder?), how it brought them together for at least a moment of mutual recognition, song, and cheerful dialogue. How applicable to Francie and Neeley and Papa are the words of the first reading of Christmas Day: "How beautiful upon the mountains are the feet of him who brings glad tidings, announcing peace, bearing good news."

THE NATIVITY OF THE LORD
TOPICAL: THE IMPORTANCE OF SYMBOLS

Betty Smith

The Christmas Tree

For the first time in my life, I almost didn't put up a Christmas tree this year. The reason? I failed to tag a tree at the Moon Mountain tree farm early in December. Instead, I waited until three days before Christmas, only to find the farm sold out and closed. So what to do? I checked out other local tree farms and they, too, had closed for the season. I still had a lot of shopping to do. And so I thought, "What's the point? The kids are gone. We expect no company. I'm not getting any younger. So why bother?"

And then a panic came over me. I realized I was addicted to Christmas trees. As long as I can remember, we've had a tree, top to the ceiling, widely spread branches aglow with lights and familiar ornaments. Suddenly the thought of our living room being vacant on Christmas day gave me a chill—the kind you might experience if, coming round a bend on Highway 1 above Jenner, you found the road washed out and your car tottering over a precipice. My adrenaline got going. Having a tree became a must, and within three hours we returned from the wilds beyond Petaluma with the most beautiful tree we've ever had—and put it up by suppertime.

Later I began to wonder why I reacted so emotionally over what anyone's rational mind would consider an optional thing of no great consequence. And all I could think of was that scene in the old musical *Brigadoon.* You know the story. Gene Kelly and his skeptical friend Van Johnson are hunting in the Scottish highlands and become lost. As they consult their map, a village appears out the mist and they enter it to find everyone in a festive mood, the men in kilts, the lassies lovely. It's Brigadoon, a mystical village that appears only once every century to spare it the violence of our everyday world.

Gene Kelly is enchanted, but Van Johnson doesn't trust it. "It's a fairy tale," he says. "Let's go!" Kelly hesitates. "I believe in this place. I can't give it up, now that I've found it." Nevertheless, he succumbs to the skeptic's influence and the next thing you know, he's caught up once more in the whirl of Manhattan where the bars are full of lonely people pretending to be carefree, where the noise and gossip of the modern metropolis prevent their hearing poetic rumors of a better world.

My malaise over not having a Christmas tree was very similar to that of Gene Kelly over leaving Brigadoon. I thought, "If I casually let go of this tree thing (or for that matter any of the great symbols and sacraments of my tradition), will I be letting go of something of immense importance to my humanity, my sanity?" My irrational but valid conclusion was, "Yes." And so, even as Gene Kelly returned to dwell in Brigadoon, I once more raised within our living room that tree that throughout my life has been my link to—what? To paradise! Because what is the Christmas tree but the reappearance in our homes every year of that very Tree of Life that stood in the center of the Garden of Eden.

Or what is the Christmas tree but something akin to that tree Betty Smith writes of in *A Tree Grows in Brooklyn:* a tree that made even tenement dwellers hopeful, a tree that grew up in boarded lots and out of neglected rubbish heaps and right out of cement itself, a tree that the landlord sent two men to chop down and build a bonfire around it to eradicate it entirely—but out of whose stump a new tree grew "along the ground until it reached a place where there were no wash lines above it" and then started once more to reach for the sky because nothing could destroy it![4]

THE HOLY FAMILY OF JESUS, MARY, AND JOSEPH

Luke 2:22–40, Lois Lowry

Gray or Every Color of the Rainbow?

A few years ago, I saw a film called *Pleasantville*. It was a time-lapse type of movie in which a current teenage boy and girl are projected back into a late 1950s household equivalent to that of the Cleavers of *Leave It to Beaver* fame. Prior to their transition the film was in color. As soon as the boy and girl arrived in that standard suburban household of more conservative times, everything went gray. And having recently watched some reruns of *Leave It to Beaver*, the Cleaver's home life does seem pretty gray. I enjoy the show; however, while billed as a situation comedy, almost every episode seems to have a moral to teach about how properly or "rationally" to run a home and bring up children.

Whether Ward Cleaver would be an admirable parent by Latino or African American or non-Anglo-Saxon standards is questionable. He's quite a Puritan and manipulatively so, as in the episode in which Wally wants to buy a suit for his first formal dance all by himself, comes home with what's a pretty square outfit by current standards but much too "loud" for Ward's taste, and is then deviously told the sleeves need alterations as a ploy to take him back to the store and select for him a dark blue suit more in accord with Ward's taste. And Wally thanks him!—as a lesson to all children never to question patriarchal authority. Gray! And there is never a mention in the series of religion or evidence of it in the home. Everything is gray and secular—the calm before the storm of the late 1960s when Beaver's generation will wildly rebel.

But the Cleaver family is still a family, a set of parents and children born of those parents. In Lois Lowry's *The Giver*, we behold a much more "improved" model of the secular family. This story takes place in a future civilization in which science and

technology—unimpeded by "myth and religion"—have achieved
a physically stable environment in which all pain and inconvenience
have been eliminated. Climate control has done away with extreme
heat and cold. There are no more pests and no variety of color
to confuse people. Everything is uniformly gray (as in *Leave It to
Beaver*). Nor is there need for the unreliable "family concept" of
prior times. Instead, to insure that they grow up conforming to
a preordained role in society, children are born of select women
called birth mothers and then assigned in nicely symmetrical pairs
to adult couples for subsequent and impersonal formation.

Infants born defective are "released" quite early, and should
any of the assigned children show signs of persistent bed wetting
or other out of control behavior, they too are soon "released." At age
12 each well-rounded graduate of this system receives a lifelong
vocational assignment. In a word, everything is efficiently done.
Feelings like anger, love, and non-verifiable fantasy are processed
out of the children around the supper table (even as Ward used
to do in the late 1950s) to forestall their someday upsetting the
productive balance of a purely material society.

Of course, shows like *Leave It to Beaver* and novels like *The
Giver* are fictional, but they wouldn't be credible if they didn't reflect
something valid about the status and trends of modern family life.
This is why the Church confronts us every year with today's celebration of the Holy Family. Old fashioned though it may sound in a
post-Christian era, the Church insists on presenting us with what it
considers a *sane* family model, the model we encounter in the infancy
narratives of the Gospels. Even back then—2,000 years ago—Mary
and Joseph had to contend with secular expectations of a family
unit. King Herod wished no more of the families of his realm than
that they breed anonymous, servile citizens. Nor did Caesar Augustus
view the families of his empire as anything but economic units,
digits to be counted and taxed.

But what kind of family model do we find mirrored in the
infancy narratives? Not something blandly secular and materialist,

but rather a family that believes in angels and allows itself to be guided by angels. It's a family that values its child not as a statistic or even a bundle of joy but as an offspring worthy to be called Emmanuel, "God with us"—an infant of profound, eternal worth and origin, unique and so much more important than such generalities as the economy or the state. It's a family hardly surprised that their child's birth should attract Magi from afar bearing gifts worthy of a king or queen, no matter that the child's father is a carpenter.

And believing itself to be living in a sacred universe, it's a family that values rituals that promote such a belief and makes use of them to integrate their children visibly and memorably into such a colorful universe—to preclude their enclosure within the whitewashed walls of a purely secular one. Yes, and here we have a family not so mesmerized by "progress" that it refuses to acknowledge the wisdom of its ancient heritage—to place its child in the hands of a Simeon and Anna as representatives of our larger human family, to receive their blessing and hear the chorus of all prior generations welcome each child conceived into this world: "Now, Master, you may let your servant go in peace for my eyes have seen your salvation, a new light of revelation to all the world!"

This makes me wonder whether this Gospel model of a *sane* family concept influenced Lois Lowry. Toward the end of her novel a boy named Jonas, bred and raised in so gray, impersonal, and efficient a future civilization, finds out there still exists an older, "backward" civilization called Elsewhere that lacks all such "rational" advantages. It's a place of snow and heat and hills and hardship, which only serves to stimulate Jonas' curiosity. And so he escapes to travel there where, upon coming—quite frozen—to the crest of a steep slope covered with powdery snow, "all at once he could see lights . . . shining through the windows of rooms . . . red, blue and yellow lights that twinkled from trees in places where families created and kept memories, where they celebrated love . . . . For the first time, he heard something that he knew to be music. He heard people singing."[5]

THE EPIPHANY OF THE LORD

Matthew 2:1–12, W. H. Auden

Christmas Comes But . . . 52 Times a Year!

With the departure of the Magi, many people assume that the Christmas season has come to an end, even though it extends liturgically through next Sunday's Baptism of the Lord—or as the English American poet W. H. Auden put it so aptly many years ago:

> Well, so that is that. Now we must dismantle the tree,
> Putting the decorations back into their cardboard boxes—
> Some have got broken–and carrying them up into the attic.
> The holly and the mistletoe must be taken down and burnt,
> And the children got ready for school. There are enough
> Left-overs to do, warmed up, for the rest of the week—
> Not that we have much appetite, having drunk such a lot,
> Stayed up so late, attempted—quite unsuccessfully—
> To love all of our relatives . . . .
> The Christmas Feast is already a fading memory,
> And . . . for the time being, here we all are,
> Back in the moderate Aristotelian city
> Of darning and the Eight-Fifteen . . . .[6]

Auden goes on to describe how shrunken the world seems, what with the passing of that more magical interlude of Christmas—how the streets seem narrower, the office more depressing. He speaks especially of a sense of disappointment, of how Christmas seemed to present us with a chance to emerge from our tentative attitude toward religion and fully believe in the presence of God among us—a chance we let slip by:

> Once again
> As in previous years we have seen the actual Vision and failed

To do more than entertain it as an agreeable

Possibility, once again we have sent Him away . . . .

But the post-Christmas blues are only justifiable if we suffer the illusion that "Christmas comes but once a year." It may come but once a year for Macy's and other commercial enterprises for whom the word Christmas means sales. But the obvious meaning of the word we use to mark the birth of Christ is the Mass of Christ, a term applicable to every Mass ever sung or spoken. So that it may be accurately stated that for some people who attend Mass daily, Christmas occurs daily—the Word is made flesh and dwells among us—and for most of us, a minimum of 52 times a year! So why the blues? Why the let down?

And if Christmas doesn't occur every week of the year, how do you explain all those dromedaries I see every week crowding our parish parking lot? They may not be literally dromedaries, but they're the modern equivalent: the vehicles whereby we modern Magi come from near and far, drawn out of the darkness of depression and the fog of secular politics by a star otherwise known as the scriptures that are read to us every Sunday. And toward what do the scriptures point us but that same old Bethlehem (the "House of Bread"), which becomes for us the table on which Mother Church gives birth to Christ every Sunday, to lay him within our hearts as in a manger, to be borne beyond the portals of our Church, lovely in eyes and lovely in limbs not his?

So cheer up! The challenge of Christmas abides. The opportunity is there for you every time you participate in the Eucharist, not only to celebrate the ancient story but to experience it, to make your own the journey of the Magi, to lay before Christ the treasures of your own personality and to receive in turn Christ himself and his capacity to dream dreams that will save you from the lethal Herods of this world and help you reach wherever you're going (as the Magi did) "by another way."

THE BAPTISM OF THE LORD

Mark 1:7–11

Mutation

Like the songwriter of a generation ago, the Hebrew author of the
first chapter of Genesis might confess, "Don't know much about
biology; don't know much about geology. . . ." But he sure had
an up-to-date way of describing the origin of our world: "In the
beginning . . . the Spirit of God hovered over the surface of the sea.
And God said, 'Let the waters be gathered together into one place
and let the dry land appear.' " He then goes on to portray first the
creation of vegetation, then animal life, and finally human beings.
In broad terms that's pretty much how modern science describes the
sequence of our evolution: life emerging from the sea and advancing
through plant and animal stages to culminate in Homo sapiens.

Despite the similarities, however, there's really a big differ-
ence between Genesis and modern science, because science views
the origin of the world as a purely physical event, whereas the
Hebrew author writes of it as also a profoundly spiritual event.
So where he speaks of God's Spirit hovering over a primeval sea,
it's not simply a watery sea he's speaking of. No, for him the sea
serves also as a symbol of chaos and suffocation. And if you wonder
why, just go take a look at the Pacific on a gray, stormy day, with
the waves assaulting the rocks as if they would chew them to pieces.
Or imagine yourself adrift at night far out in the middle of its
mindless waves, the big fry feeding on the small fry right beneath
you and you yourself likely to be swallowed up without a trace.

So when the Hebrew writer tells of the Spirit of God hovering over the sea and commanding it to back off to allow dry land and
life to emerge, he sees nothing less than God's colossal love lifting us
out of some primeval whirlpool that would otherwise suck both us
and the Garden we inhabit back into nothingness. And his purpose?

To shape each of us into an immortal and somehow immense miniature of himself.

Nor are biblical authors in general so naive as to think of creation as simply a past event. The Bible is very aware of our human tendency to go rushing back (like lemmings) into that impersonal sea from which we came. Take, for example, the people in the Noah story. Repudiating their humanity, they choose to live like predators, and very soon we find them sinking beneath a deluge of their own making. All except Noah, who, retaining his sense of justice and humanity, stands safe upon a mountaintop while the waters of the deluge recede and God has to create his world all over again—not from scratch but with the help of the zoo (and manure) Noah salvaged in the ark!

Or consider the later Israelites, who slavishly allow themselves to get caught in the undertow of dictatorial Egypt and end up gasping for life and liberty, until God has to intervene once more to lift them out of the waters of the Red Sea and direct them and all humanity toward their destiny of eternal intimacy with God and each other.

Given this Old Testament imagery, perhaps you can now see why the New Testament writers chose to describe the commencement of Jesus' career today in terms of his rising out of water while the same Spirit of Genesis hovers above him. They did it because they sensed in the arrival of Jesus a fresh beginning for the human race—the ascent (at long last) out of primeval suction of that invincibly caring human being God has been trying to create ever since Homo sapiens set foot on the earth. That's what we celebrate today: a mutation that students of evolution have yet to recognize and revere.

FIRST SUNDAY OF LENT

Mark 1:12–15, Frank Norris

Death Valley

I remember first seeing a boy coasting along on one of those light metal scooters with plastic wheels and I thought, "So what else is new?" I hadn't seen a scooter like that since I was a child, and here it was again, streamlined and shiny, but the same old toy discovered by a new generation. Nor was it long (within a week or so) before I noticed that almost every kid had one!

Desire lies ever dormant within us. We go our happy-go-lucky way, not having much but not missing much until somebody buys the first TV on the block, and before long all the conversation exchanged across front porch balustrades and the shouts of children playing in the streets go silent as each family eventually retires to its own living room to sit before the glow of its own TV set.

Desire is the subject of Frank Norris' novel *McTeague.* Its main character initially has few ambitions in life. Back in the 1890s he apprenticed himself to a quack dentist and later set up shop in San Francisco. A quiet fellow, he was now content. He enjoyed his steam beer on Sunday, kept a pet canary in a gilded cage, and quietly went about his dentistry. If he had any desire at all, it was to exchange the wooden signboard suspended outside his window for a huge golden molar "with enormous prongs."[7]

Gold, of course, was what first drew people to California, and gold is what everyone in the novel is still obsessed with. Indeed, Norris' novel may be read as a long parable about our modern secular world's concern no longer with God or one's soul (the priorities of an Age of Faith) but with material gain, symbolized by gold. Notice that even McTeague's canary cage is gilded. The character Maria couldn't ever stop reminiscing about the gold dinner service her parents once owned, nor could the local junk dealer ever stop listening. "Tell us about it again," he would say. "The story ravished him with delight."

But, built like an ox and with about as much intelligence, McTeague would have remained unimpressed by wealth if his future wife Trina had not won 5,000 dollars in a lottery. Soon the interest off that nest egg introduced McTeague to new possessions and new seductive experiences like an afternoon at the primitive movies of a hundred years ago. The sack of coins also aroused the envy of McTeague's friend and finally, when McTeague, having no credentials, was forbidden by law to practice dentistry, that golden nest egg became his only hope of survival. He does violence to Trina, steals it, and heads off for the Sierras as an outlaw.

Eventually his equally covetous and now deputized friend gets the drop on him in Death Valley. But with their only mule dead and their water gone, there's little hope for either one of them. Still, that bag of coins lying in the sand draws them into a life or death struggle that McTeague wins. But what does he win? "As McTeague rose to his feet, he felt a pull at his right wrist . . . . Looking down, he saw that Marcus in that last struggle had found strength to hand-cuff their wrists together . . . McTeague was locked to the body. All about him, vast, interminable, stretched the measureless leagues of Death Valley. McTeague remained stupidly looking around him, now at the distant horizon, now at the ground, now at the half-dead canary chittering feebly in its little gilt prison." Thus the novel ends.

Today's Gospel tells of Jesus being driven into the desert to be tempted by Satan. The Gospels of Matthew and Luke amplify that reading by indicating what Satan tried to do was awaken in Christ the shortsighted desire by which he has ensnared humanity down through the ages. Frank Norris amplifies those amplifications to show us what comes of such myopic desire—such hunger for bread *alone*. Let's hope that the example of Christ under such stress will help us finally get our priorities straight and release that canary within us from its gilded cage.

FIRST SUNDAY OF LENT
TOPICAL: ANTICIPATING LENT

George Eliot

One Obvious Form of Penance

Whenever the maitre d' of a restaurant would ask the late comedian Henny Youngman which table he'd prefer, he would say in his abrupt New York manner: "I'd like a table near a waiter!" We all know what he meant. Granted there are many waiters in the restaurant business who are true professionals and perform their important role efficiently and attentively (like my mother in her younger years and my Uncle Gene who made a lifetime career of it), what with the vast expansion of the restaurant business in these affluent times, you do often find yourself at the mercy of someone with an uncanny ability to avoid eye contact with the customer—even when the customer's pleading gaze is supported by much waving of hands and vocal tactics like: "Hey, waiter! Over here!"

It's my guess that the reason a particular waiter or anybody employed in industry or bureaucracy is inattentive to his work is his underlying wish to be elsewhere. So often in this era of upward mobility the work at hand remains secondary to other ambitions. It's done to support one's education or family. It's a necessary prelude to an early retirement. It's a way of acquiring sufficient revenue to spend on a date or invest in a less laborious future scanning the stock market. In other words, it's a job; it's rarely an end in itself.

How differently Caleb Garth approached his work. He wasn't a wealthy man. Indeed he had no knack for making a profit. He was what we'd call a soft touch when it came to money. But he loved his work—and not only his work (which was to manage several estates) but also the world of work in general. This is how George Eliot describes him in *Middlemarch:*

Caleb Garth often shook his head in meditation on the value, the indispensable might of that myriad-headed, myriad-handed labour by which the social body is fed, clothed and housed . . . . The echoes of the great hammer where roof or keel were a-making, the signal-shouts of the workmen, the roar of the furnace, the thunder and plash of the engine, were a sublime music to him . . . the crane at work on the wharf, the piled-up produce in warehouses, the precision and variety of muscular effort wherever exact work had to be turned out—all these sights . . . acted on him as poetry without the aid of the poets. . . . His early ambition had been to have as effective a share as possible in this sublime labour, which was peculiarly dignified by him with the name of "business."

His classification of human employments was rather crude . . . . He divided them into "business, politics, preach-ing, learning, and amusement." He had nothing to say against the last four; but he regarded them as a reverential pagan regarded other gods than his own. In the same way, he thought well of all ranks, but he would not himself have liked to be of any rank in which he had not such close contact with "business" as to get often honorably decorated with marks of dust and mortar, the damp of the engine, or the sweet soil of the woods and fields. Though he had never regarded himself as other than an orthodox Christian . . . his virtual divinities were good practical schemes, accurate work, and the faithful completion of undertakings: his prince of darkness was a slack workman.[8]

The reason I quote this is that, very often, when Lent comes around we have a hard time thinking up something ascetical to do, some sacrifice to make. Why not just decide to focus on whatever job or tasks we actually have to do—with all our heart and mind and soul? We may indeed discover our work to be more sacramental than we realize, a veritable rendezvous with God we've overlooked too long.

SECOND SUNDAY OF LENT

Mark 9:2–10

Transfiguration

I used to think, "How lucky Bible characters are!" They not only get to see but wrestle with angels; they get to witness miracles in almost every chapter or, as in today's Gospel story, to see Jesus transfigured and hear the thunder say, "This is my Son, my Chosen One. Pay attention to him." Nowadays people never seem to have experiences like that. Why?

Perhaps it's because we're less impressionable. I mean, now that science explains everything from aardvark to zebra and back again, there's nothing that seems to astound us anymore. We're less prone than our ancestors to see an apparition amid the shadows or hear in the sighing of the wind the lament of some ghost. Instead we go through our world the way we go through a supermarket, each pushing one's own little cart, preoccupied with one's own shopping agenda, indifferent to people around us, alert only to surface impressions, labels on a shelf. And I used to think: how sad that we've lost our capacity to see things more profoundly, to see transfigurations everywhere the way Peter, James, and John did on the mountaintop.

But notice, I said, "I used to." Because recently I've come to believe that even now, given the right circumstances, we too may witness transfigurations. It all has to do with my kid sister (she's no kid anymore). Of course, I've known her all my life. We lived in the same house until I left at 15. And you know how it is with a kid sister. Until she came along, you were the sole object of your parents' attention. Suddenly there's this other baby who gets to occupy your old crib. Then she grows up into this "bother" that lives down the hall, where she plays house with silly girlfriends who intrude on your own space to disturb the precise alignment of your toy soldiers and model airplanes. You rarely focus on her; she exists only as part of your peripheral vision. In the school corridors you dread the day when her classroom is close to yours and you have to put up with her "Hi, Geoff!" as she passes among your peers. And she has this way of interfering in your neighborhood fist fights, wanting to get between you and your opponent, shouting, "Don't you dare hurt my brother!" so that you wince for weeks after whenever your pals bring it up.

And then you leave your hometown forever to pursue a college education and ponder the meaning of the universe while she stays put, immediately marries, settles into domestic life and, except for occasional visits and chitchat about family, the gap widens— the bond seemingly reduced to a genetic link and little else.

Except that two weeks ago I received a call: "Franny's undergone surgery. They've found a malignant tumor." Bingo! Transfiguration! Suddenly, from deep down somewhere, this kid sister whom you've taken for granted all your life acquires an importance, a radiance you never noticed before! Suddenly you're shaken by the possibility that she won't be there anymore where she's always been and where (despite your distraction) you've always needed her to be. Suddenly you realize how central she is not only to your life but also to the cohesion of an extended family. Suddenly you find yourself talking to her every day on the phone. Suddenly she's a priority and you wonder, with regret, what could have made you repress such feeling, such appreciation of the very fact of her existence for so long?

You can see why my opinion has changed about the possibility of our witnessing transfigurations even in this day and age. The only thing that troubles me is why we have to wait for pain to open our eyes to the radiance and hear the thunder say, "This is your sister, my Chosen One. Pay attention to her." I certainly will from now on. I began with a Valentine's Day card (the first I've ever sent her) inscribed: "Dear Franny, this is long overdue! Love, Geoff."

THIRD SUNDAY OF LENT

John 2:13–25, Emily Dickinson

What Has Three Feet but Cannot Walk?

A friend of mine often tests my intelligence with riddles. I hate riddles. I mean, I've labored long to arrive at the intellectual complacency I now enjoy, and I don't need riddles to embarrass me, to leave me as befuddled as Alice in Wonderland in a hopeless conversation with a Cheshire Cat.

Riddle #1: A man leaves home, travels a short distance, and turns left; he travels another short distance and turns left. After a while he turns left again and arrives home to find two masked men. Who are they?

Riddle #2: Smith and Jones held a contest to see who could eat more oysters. Smith ate 90 and Jones ate 101. How many more did Jones eat?

Riddle #3: There were 16 ears of corn in a barrel. Each night a rabbit carried off three ears. How many nights did it take to empty the barrel?

Now, you may be able to arrive at the correct answers at once. Me? The first one left me baffled. The other two I took at face value. I figured Jones won by 11 oysters and the rabbit emptied the barrel in about five nights (16 divided by three ears per night). Wrong! Here are the correct answers: Riddle #1: the masked men were the catcher and umpire. Riddle #2: Jones ate 100 and won (one!), so he bested Smith by ten. Riddle #3: it took the rabbit 16 nights because two of the three ears he carried off per night were his own!

Why do riddles irritate us? I think it has to do with something deep in our nature. We want reality to be what we perceive it to be; we want words to mean this and not that. For example, one should be one and not also won. An ear should be an ear of corn and not a rabbit's ear besides! Otherwise, how will we ever maintain our sanity, communicate effectively, or control our destiny? That's why the Pope censured Galileo—because for ages it seemed the sun went round the earth and not vice versa. That's one reason why the Church kept Latin as its language of theology, liturgy, and canon law—because it was a dead language whose meanings could not change. That's why all bureaucratic and legal language is so dry and dull—out of an intentional effort to prevent any ambiguity.

But life is ambiguous. Reality is multidimensional, and our human minds, no matter how desperately we try, will never be able to comprehend the mystery of it all, any more than that child whom Saint Augustine met on the beach one day could empty the ocean into the hole he had dug in the sand.

So what to do? Stay open-minded. Rather than curse or defy the mystery of life (its being a paradoxical mixture of pain and joy, life and death), trust it. Trust the God who summoned Abraham, Moses, and Mary to step beyond the limits of their perceptions into possibilities that left them joyfully astonished. Don't be like those literalists in John's Gospel. Don't be like Nicodemus, for example, who thought that "to be born again" meant to return to his mother's womb. Don't be like the Temple leadership who thought when Jesus spoke of raising the temple of his body in three days that he was referring to brick and mortar. Don't be like the Samaritan woman who wondered how Jesus could give her "living water" since he had no bucket. They could not catch the deeper sense of the riddles he posed, nor could they sense his own multidimensionality, seeing in him only a Nazarene and not the very presence of God.

Beware of confining reality within the tight circumference of your current intellect and experience. Abide by Emily Dickinson's insight:

> This World is not Conclusion.
> A Species stands beyond—
> Invisible, as Music—

But positive, as Sound—
It beckons, and it baffles—
Philosophy—don't know—
And through a Riddle, at the last—
Sagacity, must go—[9]

FOURTH SUNDAY OF LENT

Psalm 136(137):1–6, Wallace Stevens, William Shakespeare

Finding What Will Suffice

Wallace Stevens, an insurance lawyer from Hartford, Connecticut, who died in 1955, will likely be remembered as one of the greatest poets of the twentieth century, and for Stevens, a true poet must be committed to "finding what will suffice."

We live in a world that tempts us (as it did Jesus) to think that bread (actual bread or the money we sometimes call "bread") should suffice to make us happy, or that fame and political power should suffice. But what is it King Henry says (in King Henry the Fifth, Act IV, Scene I) on the eve of the Battle of Agincourt?

I am a king . . . and I know
'Tis not the balm, the sceptre, and the ball,
The sword, the mace, the crown imperial . . . .
No, not all these, thrice-gorgeous ceremony,
Not all these, laid in bed majestical,
Can sleep so soundly as the wretched slave,
Who, with a body fill'd, and vacant mind,
Gets him to rest.[10]

But if crown imperial and tide of pomp do not suffice, then what will? Here's my take on it.

When I was about nine years old I was sitting one evening on our front porch swing on Corlies Street in Philadelphia. It was summer. Kids were playing hopscotch up and down the block of some 60 (alternate) attached houses. Radios could be heard through screened windows playing dance tunes. My grandmother sat on a rocker opposite me, while my sister chatted with Peggy Dean on the front steps. The sun must have been about to set for there was a violet, twilight tone to everything. And then, suddenly, I burst into tears.

I mean really—tears! I couldn't control myself. The sobs came from deep down. My grandmother, sister, Peggy Dean, and the other neighbors gathered around me, curious, solicitous. "What's wrong?" they asked. "Are you sick?" The crying did not subside. I found myself taking deep breaths between the sobs, only to explode again with unfathomable grief or fear. The episode must have lasted a very long three to four minutes. When it was over, again I was asked, "Why were you crying?" I was as bewildered as they; I said, "I don't know."

I've never forgotten that experience. I suppose some psychologist would trace the episode to a trauma of my infancy and would cure me of any similar outbursts by ferreting out the long forgotten experience that caused it. But, as I look back, I don't think there's any great mystery to solve. I think I fell apart (much the way Gregory Peck fell apart in the movie *Twelve O'clock High*) because I somehow sensed my world was full of violence and loneliness.

There was parental friction—a grandmother bitter over the failure of two marriages and the need to house the family of her unemployed son. There was schoolyard thuggery and the tension of classroom and marketplace performance and competition. War clouds overshadowed Europe and Asia. There was the economic violence manifest in the Great Depression. There was the prospect of a literal hell hereafter. There was everything but the one and only thing that would suffice: some irrefutable assurance that I was welcome, that I belonged, that I was not expendable but of immortal value, that what I might do or say really mattered.

And that craving for what would suffice (which in the case of true poets erupts into poetry) erupted into sobs and tears that testified to my radical need, my unconscious dream—the very aspiration that the psalmist (also in exile from the one thing that would suffice) was mature enough to express in a lament:

> By the waters of Babylon,
>
> there we sat down and wept,
>
> when we remembered Zion . . . .
>
> How could we sing the Lord's song
>
> in a foreign land?
>
> If I forget you, O Jerusalem . . . .
>
> Let my tongue cleave to the roof of my mouth
>
> if I do not remember you,
>
> if I do not set Jerusalem *[that universal city*
>
> *of absolute mercy and mutual love]*
>
> above my highest joy.[11]

FIFTH SUNDAY OF LENT

John 12:20–33, Christina Rossetti, Miguel de Cervantes Saavedra

And I, if I Be Lifted Up

At 7:30 PM, back in my seminary days, the bell of St. Francis Chapel at Graymoor would toll, summoning us to recite the *De Profundis* on behalf of the dead. The words *De profundis* stand at the beginning of the Latin version of Psalm 130: *De profundis clamavi ad te Domine* ("Out of the depths I cry to you, O Lord; Lord, hear my voice"). This is one of those psalms so familiar in our culture that writers have used its opening phrase—*De Profundis*—as a title to works dealing with their own personal distress. For example, Oscar Wilde used it as did Christina Rossetti, the latter a nineteenth-century

English poet whose ancestry, I'm proud to say, goes back to my grandmother's birthplace in Italy where a monument to her father, Gabriele Rossetti, graces the central piazza.

In her poem "De Profundis," Christina feels as down and out as the composer of Psalm 130:

> Oh why is heaven built so far,
>> Oh why is earth set so remote?
> I cannot reach the nearest star
>> That hangs afloat.
>
> I would not care to reach the moon,
>> One round monotonous of change;
> Yet even she repeats her tune
>> Beyond my range.[12]

Obviously when Christina wrote that, she was, as we might say, "in the pits," which reminds me of so many other biblical lamentations that use the same image, like Psalm 88: "My soul is surfeited with troubles and my life draws near to the nether world; I am numbered with those who go down into the pit!"

Have you ever been in the pits, gotten yourself into a hole—like the biblical Joseph, whose envious brothers dropped him down a cistern, or like the prophet Jeremiah, who wound up in the same fix? Or like Sancho Panza in *Don Quixote,* who after stumbling one night with his ass Dapple into a very deep hole saw the light of dawn far above him and "made a vigorous Outcry . . . . But, alas! all his Calling was in vain . . . and then he gave himself over for dead and buried."[13] That is, until Don Quixote came along and almost stumbled into the same pit himself. Then he heard this doleful tone: "Ho; above there! Is there no good Christian that hears me, no charitable Knight or Gentleman that will take Pity of a Sinner buried alive." Once Don Quixote was convinced (by the distinctive braying of Dapple) that it was indeed his squire calling, he went off to get ropes and laborers to draw Sancho out and restore him "from that gloomy Pit, to the full Enjoyment of the Light of the Sun."

In the Gospel reading assigned for today we hear Jesus saying, "When I am lifted up from the earth I will draw all things to myself," which echoes his earlier statement in John's Gospel where he imagines himself being held up high on his cross like the healing serpent (the caduceus) of Moses, that we may have fullness of life. And what do we see every Sunday as we pass through the portals of our church but that same Christ still up there suspended on a cross over our altar—and the same Christ lifted up as bread and wine at every Eucharist we attend? And to what end but to serve as a magnet to draw us out of the pits we've fallen into, the holes we've dug for ourselves by our harboring of resentments, our worrying, pouting, immersing ourselves in trivia—in other words, resisting the potency of Christ and his Gospel to make us magnetic persons ourselves?

Christina Rossetti continued her lament:

> I never watch the scattered fire
>   Of stars, or sun's far-trailing train,
> But all my heart is one desire,
>   And all in vain:
>
> For I am bound with fleshly bands,
>   Joy, beauty, lie beyond my scope;
> I strain my heart, I stretch my hands,
>   And catch at hope.

But, Christina, don't you realize that the strain you feel within your heart and your very stretching forth of hands are nothing but the sensation of Christ's magnetic attraction—drawing you "out of the depths"? With that being the case, can joy and beauty be so far beyond your reach, when you are never far beyond the gracious reach of Christ?

PALM SUNDAY OF THE LORD'S PASSION

Mark 11:1–10

The Metamorphosis of an Ass

In Luke's account of the arrest of Jesus we read that "his disciples realized what was about to happen, and . . . one of them struck the high priest's servant and cut off his right ear." For any modern reader of scripture, that's that! The text simply describes a scuffle between the disciples of Jesus and the police prior to his arrest on Holy Thursday—nothing more. But that's not all an earlier generation of Christians might see in the text. In medieval and pre-medieval times people liked to read the scripture allegorically. In other words, they felt that every passage—indeed, every word—contained some deeper meaning to be discovered—like buried treasure.

Take the eighth-century English monk called the Venerable Bede. He notes regarding the passage I've quoted above that the disciple struck off the right ear of the servant. Now for Bede the right ear symbolizes our intuitive ear, the one attuned to the more profound meaning of things we read and hear. The left ear represents our tinny ear, the one that catches only surface meanings and takes everything literally. So to strike off the right ear of the servant is to deprive him of his deeper sense of reality, to leave him with a superficial appreciation of life. In that context it's not surprising that Jesus quickly protests against such surgery. "Enough!" he says. And then he touches the man's ear and heals him, which to Bede says, "Jesus has come to restore our intuitive powers, our ability to get beneath the surface of things, to hear what a merely left-eared rationalist or fundamentalist can never quite pick up—the presence and poetry of God in people, nature, and events."

Listen to the way the same Venerable Bede interprets today's Palm Sunday narrative about Jesus' entry into Jerusalem. The journey begins on the Mount of Olives. Olives were a source of oil for the lamps of ancient times. The Mount of Olives therefore symbolizes Jesus himself. His teachings are the oil by which we ourselves are enlightened and become a source of light to the world around us. Jesus then sends two disciples into the village opposite the Mount of Olives. This pair represents love of God and love of neighbor, and the village represents the empires of this world whose walls Christ's Gospel of twofold love must penetrate.

In the village, Jesus tells the disciples they will find "the colt [of an ass] tethered on which no one has ever sat." This young ass is us, the human race—untamed, tied up, owned by so many negative powers: pride, arrogance, envy, fear. "Untie it and bring it here," says Jesus. And if its owners say, "Why are you doing this?" the disciples are to say, "The Master has need of it." In other words, Christ is determined to repossess and tame us, to deliver us from whatever else lays claim to us. And what happens to the beast? The text says the disciples placed their cloaks on it. That's a way of saying that once taken into the Church, we will all be beautifully caparisoned (like those steeds of medieval tournaments); we will be adorned with sufficient evangelical beauty to convey Christ's presence into every situation we meet.

Some theologians frown on this antique and somewhat subjective way of reading scripture; however, if we stay within the ample playing field marked out by our great creeds, occasional use of the method can be as edifying and delightful for us as it was for our ancestors in the faith, among whom were Jesus himself, who uses allegory in the Gospel of Mark to explain his parable of the sower, and Saint Paul, who in his letter to the Galatians interprets the Genesis story of Sarah and Hagar allegorically to underscore our freedom as Christians.

PASSIONTIDE

Mark 14:72

La Lengua de las Mariposas

It's risky for an American of my age to speak of the Truman era or
V.J. Day or that great slugger Jimmy Foxx. To listeners even 50 years
old I might as well be speaking of the Millard Fillmore administra-
tion or the War of 1812. But if I were Spanish and began to reminisce
about the Spanish Civil War of the 1930s, I suspect even young
Spaniards would react quite vividly to what I was saying. Why?
Because the political wounds caused by that atrocious war remain
fresh even today, judging by the 1999 Spanish film production
La Lengua de las Mariposas, presented in America under the title
Butterfly.

    The film is set in a small town in the months prior to the war.
Many of the townspeople are delighted over the secular democracy
that has been in place for five years. Others of a more conservative
bent miss the stability of the old monarchy and fear the spread
of anarchy and atheism under the new regime. With both sides
becoming militant, the situation is combustible, and yet life goes
on. Tradesmen conduct their business, bands play at local festivals,
young people fall in love, and an innocent, asthmatic boy named
Mocho enters elementary school.

    His natural timidity is relieved by a revered old lay teacher
named Don Gregorio. While sympathetic to Spain's democratic
experiment, Don Gregorio would introduce his students to a more
mystical vision of reality. By his own patient classroom management and his respectful way of treating each student, he weans his
students from their pugnacious ways. He begins each class with a
poem and tries to awaken in each student a sense of wonder over
the tiniest facet of nature around them.

It's when he one day describes the tongue of a butterfly that he completely wins Mocho's attention. The tongue, or proboscis, of a butterfly, he says, is like the trunk of an elephant! It's a spiral-like organ that the butterfly unwinds to tap the nectar deep within the calyx of a flower, after which it flies off to spread the flower's pollen and thereby make the world even more beautiful. Thus, the butterfly becomes a metaphor of how Don Gregorio would have his students live and behave: ever ready to probe the treasures that lie deep within reality and relay their discoveries to others. This is probably also his intent when he makes Mocho a present of Robert Louis Stevenson's *Treasure Island.*

We're never quite sure just what Don Gregorio's creed is, but whatever it is, he comes across as Christlike. To me his reference to how the butterfly drinks deeply of a flower's calyx (or chalice) brings to mind the Eucharist. And then there is a quasi-baptismal scene in which Mocho suffers an asthmatic attack on a field trip and Don Gregorio carries him to a stream and immerses him in the water, after which the boy breathes freely again. At any rate, what a mentor for a boy to have when at eight years old he's passing from infancy into consciousness!

But beyond Don Gregorio's influence there are the increasingly strident polarizations of ideological politics that break out into a war that will stereotype the once-revered Don Gregorio himself and convey him in the back of a truck to his execution. And as neighbors (to save their own skins) shout the then prevailing epithets like "Red!" and "Atheist!" at Don Gregorio, Mocho learns a new lesson: when things get dangerous, blend in with the crowd and adopt its vocabulary. And so Mocho, along with the other boys, chases the truck, shouting the same slogans, hurling stones—until, under the sad gaze of Don Gregorio, he pauses (like Peter?), stops, and, deep within himself (as the film ends), chooses (we hope) to remember someday what Don Gregorio taught him.

THE VIGIL IN THE HOLY NIGHT OF EASTER

Romans 6:3–11

Death Shall Have No Dominion

I especially remember two things about Jenny. At the classes I conduct in our local retirement community's music room she would always placidly glide into her front row seat five minutes after the hour. Jenny did not seem to live in clock time but in what the mystics might call *real* time. Somewhere in the course of her life she had acquired the pace of paradise itself, which is perhaps what made her seem so ethereal to me (afloat, as it were), not as much subject to the grip of gravity as we are.

Nor was it only her late arrival that impressed me but also the blithe way she paraded in! For Jenny was an individual parade—a pageant of simply one person—as she passed delicately through our lives always wearing a beribboned straw hat and wreathed with diaphanous shawls, clad in pastels of lavender or combinations of pink and purple, iris or rose right down to her ankles—as colorful as a rainbow, more like a child or an angel than an elderly widow. And all of this seemed quite deliberate to me, as if she were determined to live in one season only—spring—and just as determined to allow death to have no dominion. As a nurse and spouse of a doctor, she knew human frailty well; she had seen the shadow of death fall on young and old. And I think somewhere along the way she decided to confront that shadow with lavender and thereby hold it at bay while she gracefully went about her business exploring the Garden of Eden all around her.

But Jenny's pastel spirit was housed within a fragile body. One day my phone rang and a voice said, "Jenny is dying." It was early evening when I arrived at Warrack Hospital's intensive care unit. How stunned I was to see her so colorless, her breathing short, her eyes so vacant. And I thought, "So this is what happens to Jenny and, someday, to me. What's the use of all the lavender and lace we contrive to forestall death?"

But what I didn't reckon on as I left her bedside (just moments before her death) was nature's imminent intention to strike up the band, to spoil death's intent to abort Jenny's parade! For as I drove down Highway 12 toward Sonoma at sunset, a glare in my rearview mirror caught my eye. There and in my side-view mirror the whole sky had become an incandescent orange across which stretched clouds ranging from pink to rose and, yes, to lavender. Then, looking to my left and right and directly through my windshield there were enough wisps of cloud and high mist reflecting the setting sun to make the whole valley before me—in the direction of oncoming night—glow with deeper shades of purple and violet. I mean, the whole sky in every direction was full of the colors of Jenny, as if, even as her soul took flight from that frail body, she had left her whole wardrobe behind—shawls, scarves, ribbons, and skirts scattered here, there, and everywhere across the heavens in a final gesture of departure. Or could it be that God himself was laying out by way of all those splendid clouds a whole new, celestial wardrobe for Jenny composed of all the colors of the rainbow out of deference to Jenny's taste?

I experienced my faith revived. The whole panorama seemed to be a message from Jenny herself, saying, "Don't let appearances get you down. See how gloriously amid my pastels I have survived the ravages of death." And I could imagine her already somewhere on the other side of that setting sun, arrived at last in that realm of real time (beyond clock time), of which she already seemed so familiar. Jenny's son later told me that she died at 8:19 PM, precisely the moment when I beheld that sunset.

Of course, then I began to think, if Jenny died at 8:19, could it be that God expected her at 8:14? It would be quite consistent with Jenny's blithe tendency to arrive anywhere—five minutes late.

EASTER SUNDAY

Acts 10:34a, 37–43; Luke 24:13–35, James Dalessandro

La Speranza

On April 17, 1906, the Italian tenor Enrico Caruso landed at the
Embarcadero in San Francisco. He was booked to play the role of
Don José that very evening in the opera *Carmen* and Rodolfo's role
the following evening in Puccini's *La Bohème*. The welcoming
caravan conveyed him to the Palace Hotel on Market Street where
he had to put up with the greetings of city dignitaries, the clamor of
the press, and the *bravissimo's* of the crowd. That evening, however,
all who could gain entrance to the Grand Opera House sat so silent
and enthralled as Caruso concluded his performance with *"Ah!
Carmen! Ma Carmen adorée!"* that a reporter was compelled to
write, *"Something truly extraordinary transpired here tonight . . . .
This was not an opera, this was a revelation."*[14]

You can read all about this in James Dalessandro's novel
titled *1906*, which deals with the before and after of that moment
when the San Andreas Fault slipped 20 feet at 5:13 AM on April 18,
three days after Easter and five hours after Caruso's spectacular
performance. Dalessandro goes on to trace the quake's catastrophic
impact across the ocean floor and down past Fort Ross (splintering
thousands of oaks and redwoods) to San Francisco where 35,000
structures "began a violent hula dance." The jolt lasted less than a
minute, followed by clouds of dust and "seven distinct plumes of
smoke," heralds of the holocaust to come.

And Caruso's reaction? "Impossibly heroic on stage just five
hours before, he appeared as dazed as an orphaned child . . . . The
singer clutched his throat . . . 'I am lose my voice. *La voce e morta.*
Is died, my voice.'" Meanwhile, outside the hotel, buildings were
collapsing and throngs of people were rushing down Market Street
toward the ferry piers—some naked, others in night clothes, praying,

"Sweet Mary, Mother of God." Caruso continued his lament: "My voice . . . my voice ees died," and to reassure him someone pleaded with him to try it out.

And so, facing a window overlooking the chaos below, he began to sing Rodolfo's aria from *La Bohème: "Che gelida manina / se la lasci riscaldar."* Down below, people began to look up, to pause in their flight. Where was that angelic voice coming from? And there, "through a shattered window frame, Caruso appeared, his miraculous tenor drifting down, piercing the thunder and the fear. *'Chi son / Chi son / Sono un poeta . . .'* " ("Who am I? I am a poet . . . and how do I live? I *live!*"). He continued the aria, describing Rodolfo as poor yet extravagant when it comes to composing hymns of love. There was also something about his cherished dreams sometimes vanishing without a trace. How well that line befitted the situation of the crowd below as they beheld the devastation of their beloved city. But then came that thrilling crescendo that concludes the song: *"Ma il furto non m'accora, / poiché, v'ha preso stanza/ LA SPERANZA!"* ("The loss does not wound me deeply, because it's replaced by HOPE!").

May not that scene tell us something about the nature of Christ's Resurrection appearances following the devastating effect of his Crucifixion on his body and on his disciples? Does he not on Easter return to his terrified friends like, yes, an aria from Puccini raising their souls to new levels of *la speranza,* of hope for the human race? And what about ourselves, shaken as we are by political strife, lengthening casualty lists, by an absence of faith and even a delight in despair that seems to permeate some influential elements of our culture?

And so we gather now to hear the Easter Gospels once again. You may have to look far and wide for the voice of a Caruso to release all their power and buoyancy, but they remain divine arias loaded with *la speranza* for all who have ears to hear.

EASTER SUNDAY
TOPICAL: BECOMING REAL

Ghost Story

We think that first we're breathing, pulsating, living beings and that only later (after our demise) do we become ghosts. But really we've got it all backward. A good argument could be made that we start out as ghosts and only later do we become truly living beings.

Let me offer an example. If at my present age, with my already ghostly hair, I were to go back in time to confront the person I was at 25, I think, despite my age, I might feel relatively more "alive" than he. I know that, despite that fellow's youth, I would be looking at a ghost of my current self. I say this because the intervening years have taught me so much that I didn't know then.

Back then, fresh out of graduate school, my mind was nevertheless filled with the biases of my environment (or should I say the relative ignorance of my environment?). It never occurred to me, living in the North, that even in Washington, D.C., African Americans had to sit in the back of the bus. And even when that dawned on me, I had no idea of how that must have felt.

Back then, taken up as I was with myself and that blank canvas on which I was to paint the masterpiece of my future, I had little peripheral vision. I could be blissfully blind to the problems my mother was having in another city with my alcoholic father. I could barely sense the grief my faraway sister was feeling over the stillborn arrival of her first child and two subsequent miscarriages. Because I was simply not aware of them, I had no interest in the plight of people in what is today called the Third World or any qualms of conscience whenever I followed a birdbath-sized Manhattan with a nice cut of prime rib. Nor did I know what it really meant to love somebody out of anything but self-interest. In other words, as I look back, I was a zombie.

I don't mean to say that to be young is to be necessarily immature. There's plenty of evidence of people in their 20s who are way ahead of their elders (for example, those geniuses like Fitzgerald and Joyce who write classic novels before they're 30 or a Therese of Lisieux from whom I still have a lot to learn). And then, of course, there's my own son! But in my case, maturing took much longer. It only began to happen when I became responsible for the lives and happiness of others and had to seek jobs and father children and learn my limitations and care about the hurt I unconsciously caused. It only began to happen after I knew pain, after my ego began to be laid to rest. (And, boy! has that been a long funeral.)

The Easter Gospels tell us when the disciples saw the risen Jesus, they thought that "they were seeing a ghost." But Jesus said to them (in effect): "How can I be a ghost? A ghost is numb, immune to pain. But look at me: look at my hands and feet. See! I have wounds, I have known anguish; I know what it means to care. And, *therefore,* I am real—more alive and sensitive to reality and therefore more human than you can imagine! It's you, hiding here in this upper room, insulating yourself from grief, hoarding all your love to bestow it upon yourselves alone—it's you who are ghosts of the selves you could be."

According to the Gospels, we human beings are destined to lead a phantom existence until such time as we heed Jesus' simple maxim: "Take up your cross daily and follow me." Only then will we be able to exit (with him) the tomb we're already in. Only then, looking with wonder at our own stigmata, will we be able to say, "Gee! I'm bleeding! I must be alive!"

SECOND SUNDAY OF EASTER
DIVINE MERCY SUNDAY

John 20:19–31, William Wordsworth, Anne Porter, Marcel Proust

"Peace Be with You"

It's consoling to know that no matter how firmly we lock our
doors, Jesus can still break in on our privacy, bringing with him the
radiance of a divine world we've long forgotten. There was a time,
of course, when our doors and windows seemed to be wide-open,
when our senses of sight, hearing, touch, and imagination were
especially sharp to pick up the traces of God's Spirit all around us,
be it in a rose arbor or blue jay or the sound and scent of a seascape.
Or as Wordsworth put it:

> There was a time when meadow, grove, and stream,
> The earth, and every common sight,
> > To me did seem
> Apparelled in celestial light . . . .[15]

But driven by some radical anxiety, similar to that of the
disciples in today's Gospel, we learned early to bridle our senses,
to detect only the ominous instead of the wonderful in our environment. We learned to think survival, to lock our doors, shutter
our windows—to dwell within a world of business gray.

Still, even as we grow older, Christ can intrude on us as he
did on those mournful disciples. Now and again, by way of little
signals, he can appear among us to remind us that there's so much
more to reality than our doubting minds will allow—as he did with
Anne Porter, who tells of a wartime Sunday morning walk in 1940s
Manhattan with the littlest of her sons. First Avenue was empty and
gray. No one was up. The bridges over the East River stood silent
like great webs of stillness. Returning home past locked-up shops,

she paused to notice one window heaped with old lamps, guitars, radios, and dusty furs.

> And there among them a pawned christening-dress
> White as a waterfall.[16]

That's how Christ and the real world he represents can break in on us, so that suddenly we realize how much we have let death constrict our minds and, if only for a brief moment, find ourselves ready once more to share in Christ's victory over death, to explore with him once more the brilliant, eternal *now* that lies beyond our muted senses.

Marcel Proust in his masterpiece *In Search of Lost Time* writes often of such moments when, for instance, the mere taste of a French pastry dipped in tea would lift his hero, Marcel, out of the boredom of his Parisian social life to taste again the sacramental quality of his childhood village of Combray, where the discovery of a simple hawthorn bush flooded him with affection and the names of the village streets (Rue Saint-Jacques, Rue Sainte-Hildegarde, Rue du Saint-Esprit) made him feel he dwelled in nothing less than a suburb of God's celestial Jerusalem.

And then there was the village church of Saint-Hilaire, whose sculptured facade and stained glass interior made it seem like a gateway into depths light years beyond the shops around it. And its spire!

From wherever young Marcel viewed the local landscape, that spire always looked as if it were the very finger of God tenderly touching the earth. Indeed, so profoundly did he remember it that, later in life, were he to find himself in a strange quarter of Paris and to ask directions of a passerby to an intended destination and were the passerby to point out some distant spire as the place to turn to reach that address, Marcel would stand motionless, oblivious of his original destination, remembering the spire of his childhood. Only after a seemingly interminable moment would the passerby see him then begin to walk a bit unsteadily, turn the appropriate corner, but as Marcel himself comments, "The goal I now sought was in my heart."[17]

Moments of epiphany! Moments when Christ and the fullness of life he represents intrude on our shuttered world! Stay alert! Their frequency may be only dependent on how often you would like them to happen.

THIRD SUNDAY OF EASTER

Luke 24:35–48, Samuel Beckett, Walter de La Mare

They Were Startled . . .

Recently a fellow parishioner and I read parts in Samuel Beckett's play *Waiting for Godot.* He had one of the major parts while I played the supporting role of Pozzo, which required that I behave like a snide, arrogant, whining scoundrel. When I told my wife I thought I'd have difficulty playing the role, she replied, "On the contrary, I think you'll do just fine! Just be yourself."

Waiting for Godot is about two vagabonds who have an appointment with someone called Godot. Although Godot never arrives, they feel compelled to wait for him day after day. Throughout the play they sense the absurdity of their constant vigil and yet they wait. By the end of the play they finally decide to give up. Vladimir says, "Well? Shall we go?" Estragon replies, "Yes, let's go."[18] Nevertheless, the stage directions require that, as the curtain descends, they stay put.

Many critics think the play describes the plight of our modern world. Secularism has left many people skeptical of traditional religion and reason itself. Consequently, many feel lost in a meaningless universe where death seems final. And yet people can't quite give up their expectation, derived from traditional religion, that one day someone (call him Godot) may come to relieve the barrenness of their godless landscape. In Beckett's opinion, it's humanity that reaches out, while it's God (or Godot) who never comes.

But in his poem *The Listeners* the English poet Walter de la Mare reverses the situation. In his view, it's we who hide, who refuse to respond while someone called the Traveller (sic) persistently knocks on our locked doors.

> "Is there anybody there?" said the Traveller,
>> Knocking on the moonlit door;
> And his horse in the silence champed the grasses
>> Of the forest's ferny floor:

No answer! So the Traveller called out a second time:

> "Is there anybody there?" he said.
> But no one descended . . . .
>> No head from the leaf-fringed sill
> Leaned over and looked into his grey eyes,
>> Where he stood perplexed and still.

Now the Traveller knew very well that the house was full of silent listeners

> . . . thronging the faint moonbeams on the dark stair,
>> That goes down to the empty hall,
> Hearkening in an air stirred and shaken
>> By the lonely Traveller's call.

So the Traveller finally smote on the door even louder:

> "Tell them I came, and no one answered,
>> That I kept my word," he said.

But still to no avail:

> Never the least stir made the listeners,
>
> Though every word he spake
>
> Fell echoing through the shadowiness of the still house
>
> From the one man left awake . . . .[19]

From the one man left awake! So that's who the Traveller is! What an appropriate description of the risen Christ himself, for the risen Christ comes to us as someone who now stands beyond the shadow of death—beyond the grip of this nightmare we call "the news," beyond the narcotic effect of things we call "entertainment"! He comes to us as the one man who has ever been fully awake in this world and who would invite us, even as he invited doubting Thomas, to touch him and discover how much more real he is (and all that he stands for) compared to what a weary, godless version of the world has to offer.

Nor do his invitations ever cease. The Traveller of de la Mare's poem rides off never to be seen again, but that can never be said of Christ. Christ stands perpetually at our door and knocks—be it by way of a friend's concern or a good homily or a blue sky or a gentle rain or the eucharistic host or those California poppies waving to us from a roadside ditch. In infinite ways our Godot never fails to keep his appointment.

FOURTH SUNDAY OF EASTER

1 John 3:1–2, Lewis Carroll

The Lobster Quadrille

The death of a child is perhaps the most painful loss a person can experience. I seem to read about them occurring in traffic accidents almost every other week. And they all accentuate my own memory of a day in April when I, too, received a mid-afternoon call telling me my son Philip had died in his sleep earlier that morning. He was 23 years old. I didn't sleep for the next 96 hours.

Fortunately, I had the wealth of our culture's religious and literary tradition to support me in my grief. I spent nights reading everything I could lay my hands on. For what does our religious and literary tradition attempt to do—by way of Job, the psalms, and the Gospels, the writings of Paul and Revelation, Dante's *Paradiso,* and Thomas Mann's *The Magic Mountain* (especially that passage where Hans has a near-death experience in an Alpine blizzard)— but bridge the abyss of death to deposit us in a place of green fields and a city of emeralds and pearls. For example, Philip died during an Eastertide when the very name Philip occurred no less than six times during the Gospel readings—once in direct conversation with Jesus, saying, "Lord, show me the Father and I shall want nothing more." And then there's today's second reading, which promises that when I inevitably see Phil again I shall see him as he really is— God's own radiant child as much as mine.

And then there was *Alice in Wonderland,* which I happened to be teaching at the time. I found it so therapeutic because here Lewis Carroll, a teacher of logic, tries to show us how all our worldly logic is so relative. He does this by taking Alice out of our everyday world into a realm where rabbits and mice and a Mad Hatter and disappearing Cat introduce her to dimensions of reality beyond the scope of our mortal eyes and assumptions. And among her tutors are a Gryphon and Mock Turtle, who introduce her to a mystic dance called the Lobster Quadrille.

The Quadrille is danced along the seashore (at the edge of that symbolically oceanic realm that lies beyond the boundaries of life as we know it), and it requires that all the seals and other seaside creatures dance each with a lobster partner, forward, backward, roundabout, and then throw the lobster as far out to sea as possible. And as they dance they sing a song in which a whiting (a kind of codfish) invites a timid snail (symbolic of our own inclination to hide within our shells and never trust ourselves to realms unknown) to join them. The lyric goes like this:

> "You can really have no notion how delightful it will be
> When they take us up and throw us, with the lobsters,
> out to sea!"
> But the snail replied, "Too far, too far!" and gave
> a look askance—
> Said he thanked the whiting kindly but he would not join
> the dance . . . .
>
> "What matters it how far we go?" his scaly friend replied.
> "There is another shore, you know, upon the other side.
> The further off from England the nearer is to France—
> Then turn not pale, beloved snail, but come and join
> the dance."[20]

To me the song essentially said, "Don't be afraid." Don't stand with trepidation on the shore of life brooding over the emptiness that seems to await us beyond its boundaries. "What matters it how far we go? . . . There is another shore, you know, upon the other side." Since my son's death that's something I believe more than ever before in my life.

See you in France, Phil.

FIFTH SUNDAY OF EASTER

Acts 9:26–31, Alessandro Manzoni

When Saul Arrived in Jerusalem . . . They Were All Afraid of Him

In Manzoni's novel *The Betrothed* we meet a man so bad that people referred to him simply as the Unnamed. The novel is set in seventeenth-century northern Italy, and the Unnamed was a carryover from feudal times—an aristocrat who lived high in his castle at the end of a remote valley, from which he held the surrounding countryside in thrall. He was essentially what we might call today a mafia don. As the author says,

> All the local tyrants for a considerable distance around had been compelled . . . to make their choice between the friendship and the enmity of this tyrant in chief. But the first few who had tried to resist him had come out of it so badly that no one else felt inclined to make the same experiment again.[21]

And what could mere peasants do if stronger people yielded to his authority? True, he occasionally protected some people, but "more often . . . his power was exercised on behalf of evil intentions, atrocious revenges or tyrannical caprice." For this very reason another wicked fellow named Don Rodrigo asked the Unnamed to confine within his castle a peasant girl whom Don Rodrigo had kidnapped with no regard for the girl's engagement to a village sweetheart.

But the Unnamed was now an old man given to feeling "a sort of disquiet at the thought of his past crimes." He looked at Don Rodrigo and didn't like what he saw. But was he himself any different? And what lay ahead?

> "Old age! Death! And what then?" . . . That God of whom he had often heard—he had never troubled for many years either to acknowledge or deny him . . . and yet now he had moments of inexplicable depression, of causeless terror, during which he seemed to hear a Voice within his own heart saying, "AND YET I AM!"

In this state of mind it was, perhaps, not wise of him to visit the cell of his little hostage. The sight of her, the poignancy of her pleading, was all that was needed to undermine the already eroding foundations of his prior life.

The local cardinal, Federigo Borromeo, was visiting a nearby town. Even as he prepared to officiate at a service, the cardinal was informed: "A strange visitor, Your Grace." The Unnamed entered and the two men stood there, equally silent. The cardinal then apologized for not taking the initiative in visiting the Unnamed first, who, in dismay, replied, "Did you say that you should have come to me? Do you know who I am?"

The cardinal knew well who he was and there followed a dialogue in which all the Unnamed could do was reflect as if mesmerized on his long, violent past. The cardinal broke in:

> Poor wretch that you are, who are you to think that the deeds of wickedness which . . . you have carried out . . . can outweigh the deeds of goodness which God may make you . . . carry out by his will? . . . Do not prevent me from clasping that hand which is to right so many wrongs, which will perform such widespread good works, which will raise up so many of the afflicted, which will offer itself, unarmed, to so many enemies of peace.

In brief, the cardinal meant, "What's the point of dwelling on the past when you've got a wide-open future in which to behave beautifully? Think of your past as but prologue to the wonders, the moral and aesthetic challenges that lie ahead."

Do we not have in this story an echo of the very conversion the once frightening Saul of Tarsus went through, thanks to his experience of the risen Christ? And may not Manzoni's parable be even applicable to you and me? I know that—at least as far as remorse is concerned—I can identify with the Unnamed. Too often I spend my time walking backward, analyzing past mistakes, brooding over the pain I've unwittingly caused others (but really bemoaning my not becoming the masterpiece I thought I was).

But what do Christ and the Church (on our personal road to Damascus) say to us? "Hey, turn around; look ahead. A vacant canvas stands before you, as it did for Saul, ready to benefit from a consciousness more awake and capable now of moral creativity than ever before."

SIXTH SUNDAY OF EASTER

1 John 4:7–10

Rosebud

Visitors to my home often notice a framed photo of myself taken at the age of three, wearing a playsuit and standing in a brand new wagon, along whose side are painted the words "Snappy Boy." To those who pause to study the picture I always say, "When I die, my final words will be Snappy Boy," which baffles those too young to remember the movie *Citizen Kane.*

I remember so well how that movie begins. The camera focuses on an iron gate, then raises its gaze to take in a dark castle high on a hill and then on a lighted window in the castle's tower. This is the mansion of Charles Foster Kane, filled with spacious rooms and costly furniture and art, a veritable Hearst-like castle befitting a man of wealth and power. The camera continues to climb toward the lighted window, and then enters to focus on wax snowflakes falling on a miniature country home set within a water-filled glass globe. The globe rests in the grasp of the dying Kane. From there the camera rises to focus on Kane's lips, which as he expires pronounce the word "Rosebud." The globe then slips from his hand and shatters on the floor.

What an engaging beginning to a movie. I saw it when it first came out. I was about 13 years old. And though I was only a boy, that opening scene gripped me, as did all the subsequent episodes as the newsreel man Jerry Thompson went about interviewing every-one who knew Kane to find out "Who was Rosebud?" Of course, none of Kane's friends or enemies knew the answer. They were, however, able to recall throughout the movie the various stages of his career.

Kane wasn't born rich. The movie flashes back to a winter's day during his boyhood when, while he was out sledding, a Mr. Thatcher arrives to announce an inheritance and take him from his parents and their simple rural homestead to receive an education befitting his unexpected wealth. Afterward came a media and political career that left him so overbearing as to alienate all his friends and his wife as well. I remember so well that scene in which he trashes her bedroom, breaking mirrors, light fixtures, and furniture, only to stop when he notices that glass globe, which he takes with him to contemplate on his death bed.

Of course, by the end of the film the newsreel man gives up his quest to discover the meaning of Rosebud. Conversing with other reporters prior to the auctioning of all Kane's possessions, he remarks, "Charles Foster Kane was a man who got everything he wanted, then lost it. Maybe Rosebud was something he couldn't get or lost."

Well, I must say that left me pretty frustrated, but then came that final scene. Two laborers in the castle's cellar are tossing worthless items into a furnace. One picks up a sled—the sled Kane was using the day Mr. Thatcher came to take him from his rural home. Carelessly, he throws it on top of the blazing heap. And oh what a pang ran through my whole being as I beheld melting on the worn-out wood of the sled a painted rose and the word Rosebud. Why did that affect me so? Maybe because even at the age of 13 I too knew my own childhood was over, that my naive sense of the world as wonderful was about to erode before the demands of competitive survival—that that was my own sled that was burning, my Rosebud, my wagon, my Snappy Boy, soon to be gone forever.

And suddenly Charles Foster Kane became lovable to me, because in the end he seems to have recovered his recognition of what really matters in life—not wealth, not power, but love, the personal, guaranteed, domestic love he experienced as a boy, beyond which he must have sensed something of that even more personal, guaranteed, familial love of God himself revealed in today's second reading and sacramentally embodied—for Kane— in a remembered sled called Rosebud.

SIXTH SUNDAY OF EASTER
TOPICAL: PSALM 98

David and Orpheus

Old King Saul was a gloomy old soul and a gloomy old soul was Saul—until young David became his armor-bearer. For David was also a fine musician, able to pluck out melodies on a harp that soothed old King Saul's soul. Or as the Bible puts it: "Whenever the evil spirit came upon Saul, David took up his harp and played, and Saul was refreshed; the evil spirit departed from him."

Because of such references to his musical skill, David has been long considered the source of much of the music in our biblical heritage. Second Samuel actually describes him composing a famous lamentation over the death of his friend Jonathan in battle: "Thy glory, O Israel, is slain upon thy high places! O how the mighty have fallen!" And tradition has attributed to him the whole book of Psalms, all those wonderful lyrics of joy, sorrow, and hope with which we are so familiar.

But David is not the only musician in our cultural past. We are also cultural heirs to another ancient composer, the legendary Orpheus. From the point of view of our Greek and Roman heritage, it was Orpheus who introduced music into our world—music played on a lyre that had the same effect on wild animals that David's music had on Saul. Everything in nature seemed to dance to his tune. It was also told that during the voyage of Jason in quest of the

Golden Fleece, it was the music of Orpheus that quieted a mutiny and later saved the crew from the seductive songs of the sirens.

Finally, upon the untimely death of his wife, Orpheus dared to convey his repertory even into the depths of Hades. Down he went to retrieve her soul, singing, "With my song I will charm even the Lord of the Dead, moving his heart with my melody." And sure enough, according to the legend, all the watchmen of hell became entranced, the Furies wept, and his wife was released to follow his song back into the realm of life. Did she make it? Well, as we used to say when we were kids, "That's for me to know and you to find out."

It's interesting that the early teachers of the Church saw in both David and Orpheus a forecast of Christ as the ultimate musician whose Gospel amounts to the best music we will ever hear this side of paradise. And why shouldn't the Gospel be equated with music? For music is something so special. It has the power to carry us beyond ordinary talk and bickering to a level of communication that is full of heart and harmony. It changes the atmosphere around us, causing us to pause, weep, or smile instead of frown all the time.

Think of the effect of Gregorian chant echoing among the vaults of some cathedral or of Beethoven's *Ninth Symphony* or of even a simple ballad like *Danny Boy* on our minds and hearts. Music and Gospel are nothing less than the sound of love itself welling up from deep within humanity, so deep as to trace its source to the Holy Spirit, the biblical muse who orchestrates this beautiful and harmonious universe in which we live.

It's when we lose touch with that Spirit that discord happens. It's when love fades within us that the mere noise of civilization takes over: the scream of victims, the boom of bombs, and the cackle of politics, pundits, and commerce. According to the early Church, it was to dispel all such discord that Jesus came in fulfillment of David and Orpheus and all composers before and after him—to teach us how to really sing, to teach us how to become music ourselves, each of us the living lyric of a song that's never quite been sung before.

SEVENTH SUNDAY OF EASTER
FEAST OF THE ASCENSION

Acts 1:1–11

What's Up?

As we all know, Luke wrote about the Ascension of Jesus long before
we realized the earth is but a tiny planet adrift in a universe made
up of millions of stars and galaxies, so that, cosmically speaking,
there is no up or down anymore—as the inhabitants of a flat earth
once thought. So how could Jesus have "ascended" anywhere? The
best you could say is he "went out" from the surface of the earth like
a rocket ship. But where to? Some smart-aleck popularizer of
astrophysics (whom I shall not name out of respect for the dead)
once said if Jesus were intending to "ascend" beyond the boundaries
of the universe as we now know it and were traveling at the speed of
light, at this point in time he'd still be within the limits of our own
galaxy, with millions more to traverse before he reached the bosom
of his Father.

But the Ascension of Jesus was a theological insight held by
early Christians well before Luke decided to stage it as an overture
to the Acts of the Apostles. The letter to the Hebrews often speaks
of Christ's taking his seat at the right hand of God. First Timothy
quotes an early Christian hymn in which Jesus is "glorified in high
heaven." In other words, the early Church (regardless of our scientific quibbling about the validity of terms like up and down) thought
of Jesus as somehow elevated to a vantage point from which he
might rain down on the world the fire of his own Spirit—and
thereby elevate all humanity to a new level of being, endow us all
with an upward mobility more sublime than anything merely
economic or astronautic. That's what the doctrine of the Ascension
is essentially about.

But while Luke describes Jesus as taking off to disappear behind a cloud, he doesn't mean to say Jesus will henceforth be absent from this planet. If you read the Acts of the Apostles closely, you'll see Jesus quite present in the behavior of his followers. Luke's Acts of the Apostles is simply an extension of his Gospel in which people like Peter, Stephen, Philip, and Paul mime the behavior of Jesus.

For example, look at that once timid Saint Peter! Just like Christ he's now preaching bravely in Jerusalem, and just like Jesus he now reaches down to a lame man by the Temple gate "so that he sprang up, stood on his feet and started to walk." Indeed Peter's healing power is so similar to that of Jesus that even people who fall within his passing shadow are cured! And then again, we find him filling that vacancy left by Jesus in the courtrooms of Annas and Herod, who must have thought, "Didn't we dispose of this man?"

Or consider Saint Stephen, who not only preaches like Jesus but dies uttering words similar to those Jesus uttered on the cross: "Lord Jesus, receive my Spirit; hold not this sin against them." And then there's Paul, echoing Jesus in his own inimitable way, healing people far beyond the limits of the Holy Land, raising a dead boy to life, casting out demons, standing before judges in Jerusalem and elsewhere, replicating the career of Jesus with even greater potency. And while Luke offers no account of a Peter or Paul leaving behind an empty tomb, he does tell delightful stories of their leaving behind empty prisons symbolic of humanity's victory over death.

So, according to Luke, the Ascension of Jesus by no means leaves us bereft of his presence. He's with us still in everyone who has inhaled his Spirit. Indeed, Luke seems to have left the Acts of the Apostles as a book without an ending. It leaves the reader up in the air, suggesting that it's a book that's still being written—in which you may include your own life as one more extension, evidence of Christ's presence in this world.

SEVENTH SUNDAY OF EASTER

1 John 4:11–16, Edgar Allan Poe

Close, but No Cigar

In his short story "The Purloined Letter," Edgar Allan Poe's main
character, Monsieur Dupin, tells of a game people used to play with
a map. Let's say it was a map of France showing and naming its
counties, cities, towns, and villages in large or small letters. The
rules of the game were simple. One player would select a locality's
name and challenge the other players to guess what it was. Now,
normally a novice at the game might select one of the tinier localities
bearing one of the tinier, less apparent names. But the really shrewd
player would choose the name of France itself, because, being printed
in the largest letters and spaced across the whole map, it was very
likely to be overlooked by everybody "by dint of being excessively
obvious."[22]

One could say that's the very reason the religious leaders of
Jesus' time overlooked him entirely. Like the usual player of Dupin's
game, they, too, had this tendency to study only fine print, assuming
that's where they might find the answer to the quiz or mystery of
human existence. And all the while Jesus walked among them like
the name of France written spaciously across the whole landscape
of the times in which they lived.

By that I mean to say that smallness was their preference.
Their concept of God had become petty. They saw him merely as
the Chief Justice of the Cosmic Supreme Court, author of a million
petty ways of doing things, the source of minute rules covering everything from Sabbath behavior and hygiene to the limited options open
to childless widows. They saw him as narrowly partial to his chosen
people and disdainful of Samaritans, Syrians, prostitutes, publicans,
and "different" people in general. (All of this makes one suspect
that this aloof, biased, and irritable God was more a reflection of

themselves than of the original and intimate God of the Bible who walked with Adam in the cool of the evening and dined in triplicate with Abraham outside his shepherd's tent.)

And since Jesus didn't fall within their narrow concept of God and their God's way of doing things, they ultimately wrote him off. Oh yes, when he first came upon the scene valuing people more than rubrics, saying things like the Sabbath was made for people and not people for the Sabbath, when he did not hesitate to dine with a public sinner or to allow himself to be touched by a prostitute, when he began to forgive people's sins as though it was the easiest thing in the world to do, they did become curious and concerned. They sent delegations to size him up, to match him against the standards of the ominous God they worshipped and found him totally out of sync. They couldn't contain him in the old wine skins they had brought along. His responses to their three-dimensional questions had a strange, four-dimensional ring to them. And so they turned away to continue their tedious search for the answers to life amid the footnotes of their tradition.

And yet there was Jesus in capital letters, as large as life itself, as large as true God must be: caring, forgiving, healing, uttering parables loaded with grace, ready to lay down his life a thousand times for everyone and anyone—the incarnation of the only God worth believing in, a Creator of unrelenting understanding and compassion.

You know the old saying about a person's not being able to see the forest for the trees. Therein lies a warning to all of us. Never allow yourself to miss the obvious truth by too much analysis. Our creed is a simple one: God is *love*, and whoever abides in *love* abides in God and God in him—and her!

PENTECOST SUNDAY

John 7:37–39, 1 Corinthians 12:3b–7, 12–13, James Joyce

Let It Flow

The young Irishman, Stephen Dedalus (in James Joyce's novel *Ulysses)* felt called to be an artist—a writer who, like the prophets of old, would deal with the deeper issues of life and in some way improve the world. As he put it, his ambition was "to forge in the smithy of my soul the uncreated conscience of my race."

But back in the Dublin of 1904 he could find little support for his ambition. His mother just wanted him to be a nice, pious young man. His father resented the boy's talents. Only one of his companions (Buck Mulligan, a medical intern) understood him. But being an atheist and cynic, Mulligan simply ridiculed Stephen. Why should anyone want to ponder and articulate the meaning of life when human existence had no meaning at all?

And everywhere Stephen looked he saw a world caught up in the hot air of politics, materialism, consumerism, and blind nationalism—or hooked on one kind of narcotic or another, be it alcohol or money or "routine" religion or sports or a mindless job. He felt overwhelmed by this environment to the point where he lost hope. Bitterness and anger usurped the place of inspiration in his breast, until one night he smashed a chandelier (symbolic of the society in which he lived) and staggered intoxicated into the Dublin night to end up in a gutter.

Then along came Leopold Bloom, a middle-aged Irish Jew, who had been following Stephen out of concern. Bloom was a Christlike figure, gentle, caring, curious about everything, as though everything and every experience in life were an epiphany of some kind. He brushes the dirt off Stephen and takes him home. He nourishes him (eucharistically) with cocoa (called theobroma or god-food by botanists). Slowly, under the influence of this ordinary, compassionate man, Stephen's faith in human nature and destiny revives. Soberly, he exits Bloom's house at dawn to pursue his calling, to awaken the dormant world around him with his inspired writing.

Joyce uses several images to convey the effect of Bloom on Stephen. One is especially amusing but powerful. Just before making the cocoa, Bloom goes to the sink to turn the faucet and let the water flow. To its own question as to whether it did flow, the narrative goes on to reply that yes, indeed, it did—tracing the water's course from a huge reservoir far out in County Wicklow down through smaller reservoirs and various underground aqueducts, pipes, filtering systems, and relieving tanks over a distance of 22 miles until it issued from the tap!

What a wonderful way of describing what Bloom did for Stephen! His simple charity helped release that vast reservoir of love and vision that was dammed up in Stephen (even as it is dammed up in each of us), so that his creative love might flow forth even as redemptive blood and water flowed forth from the side of Christ.

And isn't what Bloom did for Stephen, what Christ does for us? Doesn't he say in the vigil Gospel for today: "Let anyone who thirsts come to me and drink. As scripture says, Rivers of living water will flow from within him"? Isn't that what's symbolized in that great vision of the prophet Ezekiel who saw an ever deepening river flowing out of the temple of Jerusalem right into the Dead Sea to turn its salty waters sweet? And doesn't Saint Paul say we ourselves are temples of the Holy Spirit, reservoirs of sweet water, of inspired words and deeds that can sweeten our whole environment—if we but turn the tap and let it flow?

THE MOST HOLY TRINITY

Deuteronomy 4:32–34, 39–40, Romans 8:14–17

The Importance of the Trinity to Me

As a Catholic born and raised and an American influenced by the
values of a highly secular society, I often feel at odds with myself.
On the one hand I feel a part of something that transcends America
historically, philosophically, and spiritually. As a Catholic I find my
sanity in my allegiance to the one and only source of our universe,
a God who, though one, is not solitary but a bundle of relationships, all of which is captured in our concept of God as a Trinity.

As such, this God offers me the most fundamental sense of
who I am despite the transient identities I carry around in my wallet.
This Triune God offers me a fundamental and divine society, a
sense of home of such durability that whatever other domiciles I
may inhabit, I will always know where I really belong, where I come
from, and where I will always be welcome—and where, since this
God is the source of all things great and small, I will never be alone
but sense myself a fellow citizen, indeed a brother to every creature,
with whom I may enjoy discoveries of not simply a scientific but a
personal nature that will take me the whole of eternity to exhaust.

In other words, this Triune God whom the scriptures and
Christ define as unshakeable love, the love of a prodigal father, offers
me a society so fundamentally solid and gracious that even death
may not overshadow its promise nor chill its warmth. And where
do I find this family of both God and the whole of his creation but
immediately in a visible Church made up of others who share this
radical view of what life and world are all about and who together
with me—as brothers and sisters—feed on the word, bread, and
wine whereby we nurture this radical sense of home and destiny?

But then I am also a citizen of a secular society that seems
to abhor the thought that I should be grounded in anything but

myself, my lonely, fragile self—a society that would save me from any system, divine or otherwise, based on the conviction that all systems, all overarching creeds are manipulative, designed to hobble my freedom to do what I please, my freedom to be "different."

Indeed, differences are nowadays so exalted and proclaimed that it makes one wonder whether such tolerance admirably values the wonderful variety of God's universe or is perversely motivated to prevent our finding any universally positive meaning to life in so disparate a world—and certainly not in any Triune God or Christ or scripture or Church. Dissent seems to be the watchword of this postmodern environment in which I live out my currently secular life, a dismantling of every so-called "truth." (And why not, since people have indeed been manipulated by so many pitchmen or ideologues who would sell them a bill of goods under the label of "truth and values.")

In essence, then, my secular world suggests that I should trust no one. We may still inscribe on our currency "In God We Trust," but that's become passé for many of the movers and shakers of our current world. But if you can't trust God or there is no God to trust, then whom can you trust—friends, strangers, Popes, politicians, the papers, science, Karl Marx, the law, one's spouse, corporations, unions? Nobody really! No one but yourself in all your enfranchised loneliness! Free at last to be lost in a world without coherence.

It's while having thoughts like this about the somewhat split nature of my psyche as a secular yet Catholic American that I thank God—come Trinity Sunday—that I'm still grounded—by faith— upon someone and something so much truer than a self founded upon nothing at all, "independent and free" (for what?) in a mute and impersonal universe.

THE MOST HOLY BODY AND BLOOD OF CHRIST

Hebrews 9:11–15, Emily Dickinson

Inebriates of Christ

The book of Daniel opens with a story about four Jewish youths who are supposed to have lived back around 580 BC. They were exiles transported to Shinar (Iraq) by the Babylonians after destroying Jerusalem in 587 BC. Now these four young men were chosen by the Babylonian king to learn the language of their captors and serve in the king's palace.

It wasn't uncommon for a conqueror to take young captives and assimilate them into their culture to fill various bureaucratic jobs. The Egyptians did that with young Moses. And I think of our own country's "Indian Schools" like the one in Carlisle, Pennsylvania, where Native American boys were required to wear trousers, boots, shirts, ties, jackets, and caps and sit row upon row in classrooms from which they were supposed to emerge indistinguishable from their European American counterparts in everything but complexion. Jim Thorpe, the All-American athlete, was a Carlisle product.

As selected aliens, these Jewish lads were privileged to dine on the very food and wine served at the king's table. But they abstained from what to them was non-kosher fare. This worried their Babylonian mentor, who said, "If you don't eat, you'll lose your ruddy complexions and weight and the king will have my head!" "Don't worry," said Daniel, one of the four. "Just serve us vegetables and water and we'll be fine." And, in fact, after ten days "they were better in appearance and fatter in flesh than all the youth who ate the king's rich food."

This story was written around 167 BC to encourage Jewish youth then living under Greek oppression to emulate ancient Daniel and his friends. On the face of it, it encourages Jewish youth to abide by kosher food laws. But on a deeper level it says, "Don't become consumers of Greek culture. Don't accept the stuff your conquerors dish out to you. Eat their cuisine and you'll soon be consuming their ideas, their polytheism, their purely rational philosophy."

There's a German saying: *man ist was er isst* ("You are what you eat"). Consume the junk food served up to you on every channel of television or radio (the commercials, a comic's cynicism and scapegoatism, the "philosophy" inherent in the pop lyrics, the celebrity cult, the paranoia of the news and talk shows, the vindictiveness of politics) and, far from your being the consumer, it is you who will be consumed, swallowed up by a culture that can chew you up and spit you out as it does all the natural resources of the world around you. Assimilate whatever a marketplace of shallow taste and ideas feeds you and ultimately it is you who will be assimilated.

Christianity supports the position taken by Daniel: "I will not be assimilated. I will not be enticed to give up my identity, my tradition, my faith in God and the sacredness of nature, and the worth and creative potential of every human soul. I will not be used and manipulated. I will not be taken for granted, reduced to a statistic or commodity."

But won't we starve if we ignore modern culture's vast display case? No, because like Daniel, we have an alternative diet to insure our spiritual (and physical) well-being. We dine at the table of Christ. Every Sunday we first assimilate his word, served up to us by our lector and homilist, and then partake of a special bread and wine that in a mysterious way links us to Christ's very being. In the process, we who assimilate Christ—body and blood, soul and divinity—and his mentality are assimilated by him. We begin to share his vision of reality. We become his body, his poetic presence in the world— ruddy, potent, a manifestation of what a free, divinely radiant humanity must be. Or as the author of Hebrews puts it, "How much more will the blood of Christ . . . cleanse our consciences from dead works."

Emily Dickinson, intoxicated by Nature, once boasted:

I taste a liquor never brewed—
From Tankards scooped in Pearl—[23]

And so say we, inebriates of Christ.

THE MOST HOLY BODY AND BLOOD OF CHRIST
TOPICAL: THE SACRED HEART

Nathaniel Hawthorne

Devotion to the Sacred Heart . . . in Context

"Jollity and gloom were contending for an empire."[24] With these words Nathaniel Hawthorne (in his short story "The Maypole of Merry Mount") describes a crisis in New England in the decades following the arrival of the Puritans, for not all of New England's early settlers were members of that austere, sable-clad sect. There were also a few lighthearted English men and women who had come to America to get away from that grim creed and had set up a village of their own called Merry Mount. Their memories were of a more cheerful England when the festivals of Christmas, Easter, and Midsummer's Eve were celebrated in a colorful manner with banners, music, dance, and costumes. It was this culture they wished to perpetuate amid the maples and hemlocks of the New World.

Unfortunately, their antics disturbed the Puritans, who outnumbered them. And so it was that during their annual Maypole celebration dour Governor Endicott entered their village with an armed band, cut down their Maypole, cropped their hair, and put their leaders in the stocks. As Hawthorne puts it, "Their foes were triumphant . . . their home desolate . . . and a rigorous destiny, in the shape of the Puritan leader, their only guide."

But it wasn't only over New England that the shadow of Puritanism fell during the seventeenth century. It also darkened Catholic France under the name of Jansenism (after the theologian

Cornelius Jansen, whose writings fueled the movement). The
Jansenists (like John Calvin) emphasized on the one hand the
remoteness of God and on the other hand the profound sinfulness
of humanity—so much so that the distance between God and
humanity seemed insurmountable. "Sure," said the Jansenist, "God's
grace is available, but humanity is too perverse to make use of it.
Even the good we do is suspect, tainted by pride and greed. As for
Holy Communion, who dares think himself pure enough to
approach the altar more than once a year! Indeed, only the most
prayerful and penitential few can hope to crash the gates of a realm
so pure, so perfect as God's heaven."

Jansenism had good intentions. It wanted to put some starch
into us, to challenge the faithful to take religion seriously. But
according to Monsignor Ronald Knox (whose work *Enthusiasm* is
a classic on the subject), all it did was depress people and plunge
them into pathological worry over the minutest of faults. Ultimately,
it left France with a legacy of joyless moralism that weakened the
Church's influence over consciences at a time when rationalism and
materialism were beguiling people with illusions of a more independent, self-indulgent destiny.

But God was no Jansenist, nor was Governor Endicott his
prophet. That point was made clear by the compassionate preaching
of such great seventeenth-century holy men as Vincent de Paul, John
Eudes, Fenelon, and Bourdaloue—and especially by the influence of
a young nun of Paray-le-Monial named Margaret Mary. It was the
story of her mystical encounters with a Christ who displayed his
heart pierced and aflame with love for all humanity that spread like
wildfire. Here was the timely antidote to Jansenism's all too severe
and intellectual concept of God: the image of the Sacred Heart, a
divine Valentine—evidence that God is not frigid and remote but
more intimate and caring than any one of us can ever hope to be.

Here was a proper return to the orthodoxy of the Gospels,
from which the feast of the Sacred Heart can really trace its origins:
"Come to me, all you who labor and are heavy laden, and I will

refresh you. Take my yoke upon you, and learn from me, for I am gentle and humble of heart, and you will find rest for your souls. For my yoke is easy, and my burden light."

SECOND SUNDAY IN ORDINARY TIME

1 Samuel 3:3b–10, 19, Charles Dickens

What the Waves Are Saying

The boy Samuel was born during a dark time in Israel's history. The nation's priests had lost interest in the God who brought them out of Egypt. They were more impressed by the gods of the Canaanites, who were so much more prosperous than the Israelites. They had begun to make of their own religion a profitable business, exploiting the superstitions of their people rather than raising them to higher levels of awareness and behavior. Israel's spiritual condition is aptly summed up in the opening lines of the chapter from which today's first reading is taken: "The word of the Lord was rare in those days and there was no frequent vision; the high priest Eli's eyes had begun to grow dim."

Still, "the lamp of God had not yet gone out." The boy Samuel, serving at the Eli's temple, was still innocent enough to pick up the whisper to which God had been reduced. He wasn't sure of the source of the inspiration he felt, but he had the curiosity to say, "Speak, Lord, for your servant is listening." And what that child heard was a challenge from God that would produce an age of moral poetry (otherwise known as Hebrew prophecy) that would forever deepen humanity's understanding of what true freedom and humanity are all about! Of course, it took a child to hear that whisper. Adults too often lose that capacity. They become deaf to any other opinion but their own, blind to any other vision but short-term gain. That was true of Samuel's era; it's true of our own modern age.

Take, for example, Mr. Dombey in Dickens's *Dombey and Son*. A prosperous, uncompromising businessman, he was much like the new railroads in which his firm invested: a kind of juggernaut, determined to push his way forward, to lay track through town and countryside, to create a shambles of the landscape and people's lives—as long as it produced a profit.

And he was so delighted when at last his wife produced a son named Paul to share top billing in the Firm's title: Dombey and Son! But how inconvenient that the mother should die in childbirth and that her son should remain so frail! How could nature be so uncooperative with the will and intent of the great House of Dombey? And why was the child so pensive, so distracted as he grew to boyhood?

Well, perhaps, like Samuel, the boy (not being suited to his father's kind of world) was more susceptible to echoes and visions of another reality beyond modern materialism. For example, while convalescing by the seaside one day he awoke suddenly from his slumber and listened. His sister Florence asked him what he heard:

> "I want to know what it says," he answered, looking steadily in her face. "The sea, Floy, what is it that it keeps on saying?"
>
> She told him that it was only the noise of the rolling waves.
>
> "Yes, yes," he said. "But I know that they are always saying something. Always the same thing. What place is over there?" He rose up, looking eagerly at the horizon.
>
> She told him that there was another country opposite, but he said he didn't mean that; he meant further away— further away!
>
> Very often afterward, in the midst of their talk, he would break off, to try to understand what it was that the waves were always saying; and would rise up in his couch to look toward that invisible region far away.[25]

Perhaps there's still some vestige of a child in each of us that, despite the material din generated by the Dombeys of this world, can still hear what the waves are saying—that despite the admonition that

> 'Tis but the noise of water
> Dashing against the shore
> And the wind from some bleaker quarter
> Mingling with its roar,

insists

> No! it is something greater
> That speaks to the heart alone
> The voice of the great Creator
> Dwells in that mighty tone!*

*A poem written by Joseph Edwards Carpenter shortly after the publication of *Dombey and Son.*

THIRD SUNDAY IN ORDINARY TIME

Mark 1:14–20, John Steinbeck

Not Always So Prompt but . . . Persistent

The Church has been compared to many things: a mother, a city built on a hill, a sheepfold. In earlier times some liked to think of it as Peter's barque designed to carry us safely across the storm tossed seas of this world toward that only port we can call home. But it has also been compared to the craft of ancient Ulysses, which wandered sometimes too close to hazardous rocks and whirlpools or whose crew let itself be seduced by siren songs of wealth and power or lolled its time away ultra-piously among the lotus eaters, or, bedeviled by Cyclopean giants, let itself become obsessed with "single issues" and, therefore, apt to apply simplistic solutions to complex problems. Yet, whatever the winds that have assailed it, Christ, walking on the waters, has somehow always appeared out of the night to set us once again on course toward home.

It's true that in today's Gospel reading Simon, Andrew, James, and John respond *immediately* to the call of Christ, not hesitating for a moment. They abandoned the nets, the many ties that entangled them, and followed him. But there are other episodes in the Gospels where, when Jesus summons people to follow him, they drag their feet and think of ingenious excuses to delay their response. In other words, they are slow about it. And insofar as that could also be said about the Church as a whole down through the ages, it makes me think of another (and not entirely negative) metaphor applicable to the Church, namely, the turtle!

John Steinbeck must have studied a turtle quite thoroughly to come up with his wonderful description of one crossing a road in *The Grapes of Wrath.* The scene takes place one summer day on a concrete highway in Oklahoma: "At the roadside a land turtle crawled, turning aside for nothing, dragging his high-domed shell over the grass. His hard legs and yellow-nailed feet threshed slowly through the grass, not really walking, but boosting and dragging his shell along."[26] Steinbeck notes how "his fierce, humorous eyes . . . stared straight ahead."

The turtle had to push itself up a steep embankment, which he investigated with head held high and then clawed and pushed his way up. Then came a new obstacle: the four-inch high shoulder of the road itself. Laboriously, the turtle shoved itself up against this parapet until its shell stood at an angle from which its front legs could not touch the ground. But its hind legs kept pushing and push-ing until the shell was high enough to plop over flat on the roadbed.

Now all seemed easy as, with all its legs working, the creature waggled from side to side—until one car just missed it, causing the turtle to withdraw its head, legs, and tail tightly within its shell. But no sooner did it venture forth again than a truck grazed it, spinning it like a coin right off the road, where it landed on its back, with all its feet waving in the air, "reaching for something to pull it over."

Somehow it righted itself and continued on until Tom Joad found it and wrapped it in his coat as a gift for his little brother. But in the end the turtle worked its way out of the coat, hid for a while within its shell to avoid the pestering of a stray cat, and was last seen walking off "southwest as it had been from the first."

The Church! Considered a slow-moving phenomenon by many, but obstinately aimed at a destination of which this world seems so ignorant. The Church! Carrying a heavy shell of tradition within which it retreats occasionally when under pressure but from which it emerges again under its compulsion to keep advancing toward its rendezvous with the source of its being. The Church! Running into roadblocks, tossed about by the violence of controversy, taken captive by forces within—like the Inquisition—or by forces without—like the tenor of the times—but relentlessly driven by the Holy Spirit to waggle on, bearing ever so awkwardly the burden of the Gospel. The Church! Namely, you and me, ridiculously slow to catch on, bereft perhaps of worldly wit and wisdom, yet likely, nevertheless, to cross the finish line by sheer tenacity if not by speed.

THIRD SUNDAY IN ORDINARY TIME
TOPICAL: THE SACRAMENTAL NATURE OF GOD'S PEOPLE

And I Knelt Down

When (as my wife and I did this September) you leave our secular American landscape, where faith has become synonymous with naiveté, and transfer yourself to a remote province of Italy (like Abruzzo, where my maternal grandparents were born), you're a bit shocked to find the supernatural candidly on display everywhere. I mean, within my grandparents' own birthplace, an ancient city situated high upon a hill overlooking a crescent bay of the blue

Adriatic, you can see a reliquary containing a thorn from Christ's crown of thorns, and I understand there are enough such thorns scattered in churches throughout southern Italy to reconstitute the whole original item!

Moreover, during our day trips into the mountainous backcountry of Abruzzo to towns with such melodiously polysyllabic names as Manopello, Serramonacesca, Pescosansanesco, and Roccacaramanico, we might see the veil Veronica used to wipe the face of Jesus (with his lovely impression still quite fresh upon it), the body of Saint Thomas the apostle, or a bit further to the north the actual house Jesus grew up in (flown in from Nazareth by angels some centuries ago). In the town of Lanciano in the company of a group of Dutch pilgrims we saw on display in a glass container coagulated evidence of an eighth-century eucharistic miracle in which blood fell from the consecrated host to quell the celebrant's doubts about the real presence of Christ in the sacrament!

Officially, the Church does not require belief in the authenticity of such relics and events. The core teaching of the Church resides within our biblical heritage and subsequent major dogmas drawn from it. But in Abruzzo people still prize this bazaar of wonders, this amazing proximity to God and the miraculous everywhere, so that it made me envy them, because, thanks to my American education, I have to analyze everything and therefore wind up before Veronica's veil not so much praying but *thinking*, "This can't be for real." And yet, I wish I could experience it as real and feel as proximate to Christ as the simple pilgrims around me do in its presence.

And just to show you how proximate to God and the supernatural people in Abruzzo do feel and *are*, listen to this. While visiting the medieval church of Santa Maria D'Arabona, I wandered into a side chapel in which a large sarcophagus stood in monumental isolation, bearing the simple inscription "Dino Zambra." The following day back at the hotel I mentioned this to my local 80-year-old cousin Rocco and immediately he bewailed not having been with me, for Dino Zambra was a fellow soldier of Rocco's back in 1942–43.

Both had been called up together and stationed near Taranto until Dino died of meningitis at the age of 23. Quickly Rocco retrieved from home a copy of Dino Zambra's precociously profound spiritual diary plus photos and a couple of leaflets indicating that Dino was already officially on his way toward canonization. I mean, talk about the proximity of the divine. My cousin's army buddy was a saint!

But I must say, as I watched that group of Dutch Catholics kneeling before Lanciano's display of that eighth-century host's drops of blood, I found it hard to be anything but an observer. I wondered how they could be so reverent (or, as a modern agnostic might say, gullible). That is, until they began to sing that old *Tantum Ergo* we used to sing so often at benediction. Remember its Gregorian simplicity? In essence, it speaks of sacramentality, of the presence of the divine in our midst under one sign or signal or hint or event after another and pleads for a faith strong enough to supplement the limitations of our senses. And suddenly I realized that perhaps more so than those eighth-century drops of blood—this kneeling, ecstatic group of Dutch pilgrims and their music was the real sacrament of that moment, the most immediate evidence of God's presence in that sanctuary. And I knelt down.

FOURTH SUNDAY IN ORDINARY TIME

Mark 1:21–28, Seamus Heaney

What Life Is All About

Driving to San Francisco the other morning, I tuned in to one of the public radio call-in shows. "Does life have any meaning?" was the question being discussed. The callers seemed to be ultramodern folk who had long ago repudiated their Christian heritage in favor of the 57 varieties of New Age "soul food" currently marketed. They were, therefore, hesitant to admit life had any meaning (possibly because it might sound silly to their agnostic peers?). The general consensus was that, while we couldn't be sure what life's all about, we should maintain the quest (as if on a health club treadmill) and try to be nice.

Living in a secular environment so divorced from the certainties of our old time religion, it's no wonder even a believing Christian wobbles a bit, doubts those old certainties, and feels lost in time and space. But should one despair when influenced by such collective loneliness and doubt? By no means, because it's just at such moments that we are ripe for some fresh revelation that can light up our day, dispel our confusion, convince us again of the validity of the Gospel's vision of what life is all about.

Take, for example, an incident told by the Irish poet, Seamus Heaney, during his Nobel Laureate address in Stockholm in 1995. A minibus full of working men was stopped one night on a lonely road in Northern Ireland by a group of armed, masked men. The occupants of the van were ordered to line up on the side of the road. One of the masked men then said, "Any Catholics among you, step out here."[27] Now all but one of the working men were Protestants and they all presumed the masked men were Protestant paramilitaries out to kill any Catholics among them in retaliation for some prior act of sectarian violence.

It was an awful moment for the one Catholic in the group; however, as he made a motion to step out of the line, he felt the hand of the Protestant worker next to him take his hand and press it as if to say, "Don't move. We'll not betray you. Nobody need know what faith you belong to." But the Catholic (almost by reflex) did step out, expecting to be shot, when he felt himself shoved aside while the gunmen opened fire on the others. The gunmen were not Protestants at all but probably members of the provisional IRA. Heaney (an Irish Catholic) then went on to say something very profound. "The birth of the future we desire," he said, "is surely in the contraction which that terrified Catholic felt on the roadside when another hand gripped his hand, not in the gunfire that followed, so absolute and desolate . . . ."

Let me paraphrase that statement. In this modern age of so much deconstructive criticism, when "cooking the books" seems smart if you don't get caught, when hatred drives young people to suicidal assaults on faceless victims, one might despair of finding any guidance that's trustworthy regarding the fundamental meaning of life on this planet—if it were not for moments such as that on a dark road in Ireland when one man pressed the hand of another to underscore their solidarity and thereby proclaim far more loudly than the gunfire that followed the indisputable fact that mutual, Christic love is what life is all about, and that mutual, Christic love will prevail in isolated fact as well as in song and story until such time as it prevails indeed among us all.

"What do you want of us, Jesus of Nazareth? Have you come to destroy us?" cry the adamant partisans of today's world, possessed to the point of violence. To whom Jesus might reply, "Yes, not by your kind of violence, by squeezing a trigger, but by the mere squeeze, the exorcizing contraction of my gracious hand on yours. Can you bear to experience that kind of 'violence'?"

As for me, one thing I know! Having read that story told by Seamus Heaney, I will never again press the hand of my neighbor at the Eucharist during the sign of peace without recalling to the very soles of my feet what Christic life is all about.

FIFTH SUNDAY IN ORDINARY TIME

Job 7:1–4, 6–7, Mark 1:29–39

"Comedy Is Not Anarchic; It Is a Defender of a More Human Order" (William Lynch)

How many of us can identify with today's first reading? Life is a bore, the same darned thing day after day, sheer monotony. Will I ever see happiness again?

Many years ago, as I sat with 300 other seminarians in the semicircular auditorium of the Gregorian University in Rome listening to a lecture by Father Tromp on the nature of the Trinity, I caught—out of the corner of my eye—some movement in the balcony that stretched along the front of the hall and over the high dais and lectern where Father Tromp was speaking. Now you have to realize these 300 seminarians came from every nation under the sun. There were Germans in red cassocks, Frenchmen in blue sashes, Scots in the color of heather, Brazilians in green piping, Africans and Asians, all of whom were wearily trying to follow Father Tromp's monotonous discourse.

But obviously they too saw what I saw, for now all eyes were raised to that balcony where the figure of an American seminarian had sidled along until he stood directly over the unsuspecting Father Tromp. This seminarian then produced a cup of soapy water and a bubble pipe and began to do you know what. Just at that moment Father Tromp had lifted his head and hand to make a point when down before him there fell a continuous flow of glistening, rainbow-hued bubbles. He paused and looked up. We held our breath. And then the whole chamber roared with laughter. That seminarian had brought us all down to earth, having probably been inspired by the Trinity itself to do so, since Father Tromp was having a terrible time explaining it to us in the first place.

There were other such incidents, as when in the midst of a lecture on the Church in that same vast auditorium a somewhat groveling member of some religious order, carrying an armful of books, came in late, slamming the door. As he passed right in front of the lecturer, he dropped all the books on the floor and spent all of three minutes trying to gather them up—only to drop the armful twice more with much clatter before reaching his seat high in the hall's back row. We learned later that he was no member of a religious order at all but some wag from the English College out to break up the monotony of the class.

Breaking the monotony! That's what humor does, nor do I think we fully realize the redemptive importance of such humor in our lives. Of course, I don't mean ridicule, for ridicule is not funny but the product of a mean streak characteristic of people too serious for their own good, like Bible-thumpers and ideologues. And why are they always so serious? Because they've got everything figured out and are not amused if contradicted. Monotonously "correct" in their approach to life, they have no tolerance for its often-hilarious complexity.

In today's Gospel reading Jesus says he wants to move beyond Capharnaum to deliver Good News, "tidings of joy" to people far and wide—in other words, to blow rainbow-hued bubbles like my seminarian friend, to disturb the monotony of pharisaical religion, to exorcise the demons that keep us in the kind of funk expressed by Job in today's first reading. His disciples will soon prove that they have a much more serious political agenda for him to pursue and already want to manage his movements. The result? They will have no little share in the efforts of humorless scribes and Pharisees to turn what was meant to be a divine comedy into a tragedy. A humorless world not in the least amused by the multi-dimensionality of Christ and his vision of life will kill him, expel him from this world's auditorium.

Except, come Easter, we'll all know who had the last laugh!

SIXTH SUNDAY IN ORDINARY TIME

Mark 1:40–45, Leo Tolstoy

Moved with Anger, Jesus Stretched out His Hand

Anna Karenin had succumbed to the charms of a liberally minded and handsome Russian army officer named Vronsky during their brief encounter on a train from Moscow to St. Petersburg. Leo Tolstoy writes of her with compassion in his novel bearing her name. After all, she was a still very attractive woman whose need for love went unnoticed by her husband—20 years older than she and a numbers-crunching bureaucrat who married her more out of sense of "Well, it's about time I married" than out of any real affection. And so Anna was quite vulnerable when Vronsky put the moves on her.

Now this was way back in the 1870s in the mostly conservative Russia of the czars and, while adultery was not uncommon among the aristocracy, you didn't parade it about in public. But Anna was as honest as she was passionate and, finding it unbearable (after giving up her husband) to remain cooped up in a hotel while Vronsky (as a male) could go about as he pleased, she chose one evening to defy those who shunned her and boldly attend the theatre in the company of a notorious princess.

Her lover winced at the thought and tried to prevent her, no doubt worried about the negative attention it might bring to him! He was angry at her refusal to realize her position. He wanted to say, "For you to appear at the theatre in that dress, accompanied by the princess who is only too well known to everyone is equivalent not merely to acknowledging yourself a fallen woman but to throwing down the gauntlet to society, that is to say, cutting yourself off from it forever."[28]

But that's what she did. She sat in a box exposed to an audience that was a microcosm of St. Petersburg society—the "dirty crowd" in the gallery, the bourgeoisie in the boxes and the aristocrats in the front boxes who stood out as the elite of the social hierarchy. Vronsky followed her, keeping his distance of course, and noticed the scorn with which Anna was treated by a woman in the box next to her and watched her soon return to the security of her hotel. There he found her "still in the same dress as she had worn at the theater . . . staring straight before her." He could only say, "I begged, I implored you not to go. I knew it would be unpleasant . . . ." To which she emotionally replied, "Unpleasant! It was awful! As long as I live I shall never forget it. She said it was a disgrace to sit beside me."

We live in a world where the mistakes of many are compounded by the cruelty of the righteous. Would Jesus have considered it a disgrace to sit beside Anna? The Gospels offer evidence that he would not. Indeed, he might prefer it to being hosted by the self-righteous. Nor is it only the sinner who is ostracized by human societies but anyone who may be of a different complexion or creed or income level or health status, as in the case of the leper in today's Gospel who really represents all those whom we treat as "lepers" regardless of their medical condition.

Such victimization is high on Jesus' agenda for reform and that becomes quite clear in today's episode in which, according to many scholars, our text should read Jesus "was moved with anger" and not simply pity—an anger still evident in the stern way Jesus sends the leper off to have his cure certified by a priest. And why anger? Because Jesus and God must occasionally get fed up with the way we treat each other, abusing those who are vulnerable to begin with and dividing society into clean and unclean when as a matter of fact we are all vulnerable, ill and in need of healing in so many ways.

Indeed, if you read the Gospel of Mark closely you will get the impression that Jesus' entry into Galilee was akin to the Allied landing on D-day! His mission was an assault on the legion of demons that possess us and especially that demon of self-righteousness, which has caused so much needless suffering to the so-called "misfits" of this world.

SEVENTH SUNDAY IN ORDINARY TIME

2 Corinthians 1:18–22, James Joyce

Amen

Scripture tells us that the redemption of the world depends on our ability to utter the magic word "yes," which in Hebrew is "amen." Until we can say that with vigor, we'll never be fully alive. According to the Bible, Abraham seems to have been the first person to get the word out. He came from a long line of naysayers: Adam, Eve, Cain, Lamech, the Babylonian tower builders, and so on. Their approach to life was wary, quick to negate God, people and things. Abraham had good reason to be somewhat negative himself, for he and his wife were old and childless, with nothing to look forward to. Yet God confronted him with a challenge one day: "Leave your country and kindred, all that's familiar to you, and go to the land I will show you." And the good book says, "Abraham *hay-amin.*" He said, "Amen, yes!" And miracles began to happen.

But Abraham's descendants were not quite able to maintain his affirmative approach to life. We find them 400 years later merely surviving in Egypt as complacent slaves. Yet again a man named Moses, loyal to the affirmative memory of Abraham, stimulated them to depart from Egypt in quest of an impossible Promised Land. And Exodus says of them as they stood liberated on the farther shore of the Red Sea, "they felt reverence for the Lord and *ya-aminu* . . . they said amen, yes, yes indeed!"

Still, once the Israelites were settled in that Promised Land, negativity resurfaced. They lost their spirit of adventure so that the prophet Isaiah had to scold them: "If you do not *ta-aminu,* give a firm amen or yes to God and life, you will wither away."

But the prophets proved not very effective in cultivating humanity's ability to say "yes" instead of "no" or "maybe" to life. So along came Jesus. Here was a man who was absolutely affirmative, absolutely imaginative, doubtless about the power of mercy and love. His "yes" to life and creation was so absolute that Saint Paul simply calls him God's "yes" to us—and the commencement of humanity's enduring "yes" to God. Read it in 2 Corinthians: "The Son of God, Christ Jesus, whom we preached to you, you have not found wavering between yes and no. With him it has always been amen—yes, for to all the promises of God he supplies the yes—amen that confirms them. That is why we utter yes—amen through him to the glory of God."

According to Paul, Christ's "yes" to life is so genuine and potent, it's contagious and resounds down through history even to this very moment and the Eucharist when, in response to the priest's eucharistic prayer we all sing out Christ's invincible "amen"—"yes" to life and each other, hopefully with all our hearts—in the manner of Molly (Marion) Bloom (born on the feast of Mary's Nativity and, therefore, a symbol of that affirmative Mary, spouse of the Holy Spirit and mother of us all) in James Joyce's novel *Ulysses*.

Read the novel's closing lines, which are also the closing lines of Molly's famous soliloquy as she lies in bed contemplating her life and our rich, diverse world of crimson seas and sunsets and rose gardens and her own self as a mountain flower—a soliloquy punctuated not by periods, commas, or question marks, but rather (like a river of life) by Molly's own yes, yes, yes, all of which esscalate into one grand, final Yes! Amen.

EIGHTH SUNDAY IN ORDINARY TIME

Hosea 2:16b, 17b, 21–22, Eudora Welty

God's Covenant of Love: An Incarnate Example

Far out in the country one cold December day a very old black woman, wearing a red bandanna and long dark dress was walking along a path through the pinewoods. Her name was Phoenix Jackson. She had a little cane and as she made her way through the wintry Mississippi landscape she would say, "Out of my way all you foxes, owls . . . jack rabbits . . . and wild animals! . . . I got a long way."[29] On she went, up steep hills and through thorn bushes and over a log thrown across a creek. "I wasn't as old as I thought," she said, having managed that. Then she passed through a barbwire fence and across a misty field of tall, dead cornstalks until she reached a road.

Once on the road, she stumbled into a ditch and lay there on her back like a June bug until a hunter lifted her out and said, "Well, Granny . . . you take my advice and stay home." But on she went until she reached the streets of Natchez, which were strung with red and green Christmas lights and full of perfumed Christmas shoppers. Phoenix passed them to enter a big building, climb its staircase, and enter a doctor's office.

"Aunt Phoenix," said the nurse. "Is your grandson's throat any better since the last time you came for the medicine?" The boy had swallowed lye some years earlier and he would not heal. "My little grandson, he sit up there in the house all wrapped up, waiting by himself. We is the only two left in the world. He suffer but it don't seem to put him back at all. He got a sweet look. He going to last. . . . I not going to forget him again, no, the whole enduring time. I could tell him from all the others in creation." The nurse gave Phoenix some medicine and a nickel as a Christmas charity. Phoenix went out and bought her grandson a paper windmill on a stick. "I'll march myself back where he waiting, holding it straight up in this hand."

Eudora Welty called this story "The Worn Path." It's a story about love—not romantic love or cold, efficient charity but the kind of love that rises from somewhere just below your heart and compels you to go that extra mile, to be devoted to someone whom no one else in this world might even notice. And what if Phoenix Jackson's grandson is dead? Readers asked Eudora Welty that and she replied, "What if he is?" Old Phoenix would make that same journey (as pilgrimage?) again and again if only to keep alive a sense of her grandson's existence, of her relationship to what had become for her a pearl of great price. Phoenix Jackson, by way of her grandson, had developed a habit of fidelity she could never lose.

This story says a lot to me, having had a child who was also ill, afraid of this world and therefore given to ways of escaping it, like becoming addicted to drugs in his teens. And I followed my own worn path (as parents do) back and forth to the city, up the Waldo Grade, across the Golden Gate, looking for him, finding him, losing him, tutoring him, sheltering him, enjoying him with a breakfast here, a movie there, discovering in him things that made my journey less and less a "paternal obligation" and more and more a compassionate delight.

Nor has his death ever stopped the momentum of the "Phoenix Jackson" fidelity, the covenantal love I feel for him. I still make the trips and visit the familiar streets to place a rose on a doorstep or by a hotel entrance. It's something I'm driven to by an experience of awe and love that must be familiar to each of you. And again, it's not romantic, it's not duty, it's not charity. It's rather a surge such as Jesus must have felt when in the Gospel it says, "He was driven by the Spirit"—an upwelling that compels us wonderfully and in the face of death itself to walk the walk of dedication and delight.

NINTH SUNDAY IN ORDINARY TIME

2 Corinthians 4:6–11, Oscar Wilde

To Reveal Means to Unveil

Dorian Gray kept a veil over the portrait of himself done by the artist Basil Hallward. It had been painted when Dorian was in the prime of his youth, possessed of a unique beauty. Now while the artist was still in the process of completing it, he allowed the debonair Lord Henry Wotton to view it. "Basil," he said, "this is extraordinary! I must see Dorian Gray."[30] This made Basil uneasy. He knew Lord Henry to be a cynic, a nihilist, a man with no regard for traditional moral standards and beliefs, and so he pleaded, "Dorian Gray is my dearest friend . . . . He has a simple and beautiful nature . . . . Don't spoil him . . . . Your influence would be bad." But influence him he did!

Over time he advised Dorian not to become the "echo of someone else's music, an actor of a part that has not been written for him. The aim of life is self-development . . . . People are afraid of themselves, nowadays. They have forgotten the highest of all duties, the duty that one owes to oneself . . . . The terror of society, which is the basis of morals, the terror of God, which is the secret of religion—these are the two things that govern us. And yet . . . I believe that if one man . . . were to give form to every feeling, expression to every thought, reality to every dream . . . we would forget all the maladies of medievalism . . . . The only way to get rid of temptation is to yield to it."

You know the story. Dorian succumbed to Lord Henry's Byronically romantic notion of "Do your thing and to hell with what people think." He became self-indulgent and fatally insincere in his relationships, all of which (according to Oscar Wilde) began to tarnish his soul, of which Dorian became aware when one evening upon returning to his bedroom his eyes fell on his portrait. "He started back in surprise . . . . In the dim arrested light . . . the face appeared . . . changed . . . . One would have said that there was a touch of cruelty in the mouth . . . . He rubbed his eyes, and came close . . . there was no doubt that the whole expression had altered . . . . The thing was horribly apparent." He decided to veil the portrait from view, for somehow it had begun to mirror his soul.

Thereafter, while Dorian, despite the passage of time, remained as youthfully handsome as ever, the painting deteriorated day by day so that in the end, unable to bear the sight of it, he stabbed it. Summoned by Dorian's servants, the police broke into his room to find a hideous Dorian lying on the floor lifeless from a stab wound, while on the wall they beheld his portrait, its features restored to their original "youth and beauty."

A gripping if melodramatic tale which Hollywood has capitalized on several times! But I dwell on it here because I find in it a reverse analogy to some of Saint Paul's imagery in 2 Corinthians. In chapter three he tells of how Moses kept a veil over his face—just as Dorian kept one over his portrait. But the veil in Moses' case was not meant to hide something monstrous but to spare his people the radiance his face derived from looking upon God on Mount Sinai. The splendor would have been too much for them to bear. But Moses' splendor was a fading splendor to be one day superseded by the unveiled splendor we, as Christians, are to exhibit to the world, thanks to our inhabitation by Christ and his Spirit. We have become, says Paul, like mirrors reflecting the splendor of God. No, more! We have been transfigured into his likeness "from splendor to splendor; such is the influence of the Lord who is Spirit." Indeed, we are now a "new creation," for God, who (way back in Genesis) said, "Out of darkness, let light shine," has caused his light to shine within us; has unveiled "the glory of God in the face of Jesus Christ" by way of our own Christic countenances.

So, laying aside such grim stories as that of Dorian Gray, why don't we all begin to greet one another with smiles reflective of that transfiguring Spirit within us—smiles reflective of souls that, whatever our actual age may be, God wills to be forever young and beautiful.

TENTH SUNDAY IN ORDINARY TIME

Genesis 3:9–15

Remembering

My memory prior to age five is pretty vacant. There's an impression of a parlor decorated for Christmas, there's the echo of a bell announcing the arrival of an ice cream vendor, there's a partially completed picture puzzle featuring men in bright red hunting jackets, and then there are flickering images of a movie scene that has haunted me all my life.

I can only assume my mother had decided to take me with her to a Saturday matinee despite my tender age. Whatever the circumstances, I remember the screen's image of a young man in a roadster driving down a narrow road behind a two-door coupe driven by a woman. The young man is frantic because he can see that a truck, parked on a hill, has lost its brakes and begun to roll toward the road. Try as he might, he can't get the attention of the woman who stares stonily ahead. Then comes a terrific collision. The truck crushes the coupe. The woman dies.

In all the subsequent years of my more conscious existence, that scene kept coming back to me. It returned in moments of idleness, isolated from any fuller remembrance of the circumstances in which I first beheld it. Indeed, there have been times when I wondered whether it was a morbid product of my own imagination. And then along came cable with its old movie channels and I thought, "Maybe that scene will pop up one day in some TV revival." It never did. Of course, what were the odds that would happen? A million to one? I mean we're talking about one scene out one movie out of all the films made between 1928 and 1934. And we're assuming that, if the movie still existed and a movie channel actually selected it to be shown in the course of a year, I would be present at that precise moment to catch it. Not likely!

But then! On a Friday in April of 2001, while wasting some time before supper, I turned on an old movie channel. A 1933 W. C. Fields feature was ending, to be followed by one of those old Saturday matinee shorts. I watched it casually, not even stimulated by its topic of mental telepathy. A young man, having overslept, is groggily preparing to go to work. He pays passing notice to his mother's photo on his dresser and then descends to his roadster and pauses. He thinks he hears his mother's voice, saying, "John! John!" But she's in faraway Chicago. He dismisses the thought and goes to start his car and realizes he has left his key by his mother's picture on the dresser. Irritated, he goes back for it and then sets off to work. (Ho hum!)

Now, he's driving through a residential area and out onto a narrow highway. (I sat up on the couch!) Ahead of him was a gray coupe driven by a woman in a bell shaped hat. ("This is it!" I shouted, leaping to my feet.) At the top of a hill a truck's brakes give way and down it comes. The young man looks helpless. The truck smashes the coupe. A crowd gathers around the woman lying dead on the road. The young man realizes he was spared the same fate by the delay initiated by what he thought was his mother's voice. But what moved me more than my recovery of the film's actual story or theme was how—after 68 years—all the pieces of a puzzle had come together for me around the one piece I had retained. In some small way, I felt fulfilled.

Some theologians use amnesia or forgetfulness to explain the plight of our human race. Somewhere (they say) back at the time of our collective origin, we forgot our relationship with a truly personal Creator and wandered off, like Adam and Eve and Cain, to make our way independently in this world. The consequence? This nightmare we call "the news of the day." But that's where the

Church, the Bible, and the sacraments come in, because their whole
intent is to heal our amnesia, to play back for us the *whole, radically
comprehensive* story of humanity without which we hold but a
few pieces of the human puzzle—a consciousness beset with aggra-
vating vacancies that keep even philosophers awake at night.

ELEVENTH SUNDAY IN ORDINARY TIME

Mark 4:26–34, Theodore Dreiser

A Sigh Is Still a Sigh

An acquaintance of mine recently informed me that his 21-year-old
son wants something. He said this with great relief. His son had
been experimenting with drugs in junior high school. By the time
he was 16 he was an addict, alienated from everyone, apathetic,
having no interest in life or this world. Now he has begun to want
things. He wants legitimate access to money. He wants to move
from a hotel in the Tenderloin to a hotel or cheap apartment in a
better environment some blocks away. He wants a microwave oven
so he can eat cooked food cheaply in his own place. He doesn't
yet desire a thing like complete "recovery." His low self-esteem
prevents him from hoping for a warm relationship with a woman.
He doesn't dream of having a family of his own or a college education or a career or anything so grand as a life of service to others.
But he wants something ever so minimal—and that's a sign of life.

    Redemption can be a relatively slow process for all of us,
and it has something to do with being able to want things, to wish.
Theodore Dreiser in his novel *Sister Carrie* tells of a younger sister
of a Midwestern family who leaves her small town for Chicago at
the turn of the century. Dreiser's account of her odyssey is very
compassionate because he had a couple of sisters who "disgraced"
the family by doing the same thing.

Carrie had no clear idea of what she wanted in the big city except to escape the poverty and boredom of her rural life, to better herself materially. She wanted money, of course. She had no qualms about that. As Dreiser puts it, money was to her simply something everybody else had and she must get. She wanted nice things to wear. "Fine clothes to her were a vast persuasion; they spoke tenderly and Jesuitically for themselves. When she came in earshot of their pleading, desire in her bent a willing ear."[31] When a gentleman friend pointed out the stylish women who carried themselves with sophistication and grace, "she felt a desire to imitate it." When taken for a late afternoon carriage ride along North Shore Drive she was impressed by the mansions built there. "Across broad lawns . . . she saw lamps faintly glowing upon rich interiors. . . . She was perfectly certain that here was happiness."

Now, we might righteously intervene here to remind Carrie that the objects of her desires are petty things, of little eternal worth. We might lecture her on the lasting value of higher, spiritual things. But we'd be missing Dreiser's point. It's not so much what Carrie desires but the fact that she desires it, that she has wishes, hopes. "We live by hope," says Saint Paul. Desire is synonymous with life.

And God is a patient cultivator of desire, of life. True, we hear of saints who as children were precociously drawn to God directly and transcended all other desires. But with most of us God entices us by intermediate steps, attracting us from one thing to another, from a room in the Tenderloin to a room several blocks away, from one level of consciousness to another, until we reach a threshold where we long not so much for things but simply to be in the deepest sense of the word, which is ultimately of course to be like Christ. First comes "the blade, then the ear, then the full grain in the ear."

At the end of Dreiser's novel, Carrie has attained fame and fortune as an actress. She has literally reached the top: she lives in a penthouse in New York. But her desire is still strong and unfulfilled. There was something else out there she had to have; it seemed her life was ever meant to be "the pursuit of that radiance . . . which tints the distant hilltops of the world."

TWELFTH SUNDAY IN ORDINARY TIME

2 Corinthians 5:14–17, Lewis Carroll

The Wood with No Names

The prophet Isaiah once foresaw a world in which "the wolf shall dwell with the lamb, and the leopard shall lie down with the kid and the calf and the lion together, and a little child shall lead them." It was a vision of what has been called the "Peaceable Kingdom"—a world in which all the old fears and hostilities that have afflicted humanity since our loss of Eden will have passed away—a world in which that old solidarity between humanity and nature that marked paradise will have been restored. "And the cow and the bear shall feed together and the weaned child shall put his hand in the adder's den, nor shall they hurt or destroy in all my holy mountain, for the earth shall be full of the knowledge of the Lord as the waters cover the sea."

An impossible dream! And yet we keep running into it in literature. For example, little Alice experiences something of the same vision in Lewis Carroll's *Through the Looking Glass*. Very soon after she passes through that mirror over her mantle piece and wanders into the strange chessboard landscape behind the Looking Glass House, she crosses a brook and finds herself confronted by a very dark wood. "This must be the wood," she thought, "where things have no names. I wonder what'll become of my name when I go in?"[32] Sure enough, as soon as Alice entered the wood, she enjoyed its coolness and said what a comfort it was "after being so hot, to get into the—into the—into *what*? . . . I mean to get under the— under the—under *this*, you know!" And she put her hand on the trunk of a tree. Nor could she then remember her own name. (The world around her had been washed clean of all the tags humanity has placed on things down through its long and fretful history.)

Just then a Fawn approached and together they walked along with Alice's arm draped lovingly around its neck—until they began to exit the other side of the wood. Then, "I'm a Fawn!" cried her companion. "And, dear me! you're a human child!" A sudden look of alarm came into the Fawn's beautiful brown eyes, and in a moment it darted away at full speed. They were back again in that world of tags by which we superficially define things and one another. They were back again in that world of name-calling, of those often silly but lethal distinctions by which we sort out the desirable from the undesirable in this world: Asian, European, Arab, Jew, Black, White, Catholic, Protestant, rich, poor, migrant, native born, sweet, sour—ad infinitum and ad nauseam.

The Church is supposed to be that Peaceable Kingdom that Isaiah foresaw or a "wood with no names" such as Alice encountered. Like Alice, we too have crossed a baptismal brook (the River Jordan, to be exact). We too have entered a Promised Land of new, Christic values. Having done so, we are expected to shed all those tags and demographics by which the Caesars of this world would define us. We are expected now to recognize our mutual solidarity with everyone and everything in this universe. Saint Paul says as much in the second reading for today. How does he put it? "From now on we regard no one according to the flesh . . . . For whoever is in Christ is a new creation: the old things have passed away."

Welcome then to the Peaceable Kingdom, to a world of benign amnesia in which all our old biases and festering resentments are meant to be forgotten, to yield to the remembrance of who we really are: the gracious offspring of a gracious God and caretakers of this garden we call earth.

THIRTEENTH SUNDAY IN ORDINARY TIME

Mark 5:21–43, Dorothy Parker

Sleeping Beauty

Today's Gospel episode about a young girl whom Jesus raises from a deep sleep brings to mind all those Sleeping Beauty stories that have become a part of our culture (for example, the one we rarely hear about in the book of Tobit). That's one not so much about a girl gone comatose but about one—named Sarah—who was victimized by a jealous demon named Asmodeus. This demon had already strangled seven successive husbands who dared approach her on their wedding night, so that what began as a tragic predicament was fast becoming a joke. After a seventh night of frustration, Sarah's maids could hardly repress their mirth over her plight.

But every such story has a prince. In Sarah's case, it was her distant cousin Tobias with the angel Raphael. Raphael encouraged Tobias to wed Sarah and advised him on how to deal with the demon. So on their wedding night (even while Tobias's diffident father-in-law was digging an eighth grave in the backyard) Tobias placed the heart and liver of a fish on some burning embers. Hardly an aphrodisiac, the smell nevertheless drove Asmodeus all the way to Egypt, never to return. Sarah was at last free to experience fulfillment.

Now this story, like all stories, has its deeper meaning. The heart and the liver were considered to be the seat of intellect and feeling in ancient times. Possession by Asmodeus could symbolize Sarah's repression of her own intellect and emotions, making her toxic to be with. But Raphael's "heart and liver magic" does the trick: it revives her timid intellect and emotions to release her creative capacity.

As such, Sarah could be a symbol for all women down through the ages, who, because of male dominion, grew up abused and disenfranchised—all the while longing for release, longing to be in the fullest sense of the word. Perhaps it's that hope that underlies all such Sleeping Beauty stories: Snow White; Dorothy, who fell asleep in that field of poppies in *The Wizard of Oz;* Briar Rose, who fell into a deep sleep of a hundred years, hedged in by an impenetrable tangle of thorns. And then, again, there's today's New Testament account about Jairus' nubile daughter, seemingly dead to the world, surrounded by professional mourners who impeded all access to her until Jesus came along. Of course these stories may also symbolize the repression of the feminine in men as well, insofar as the feminine has long been a metaphor for heart, sensitivity, intuition, things men are often too shy to express.

However you take it, the stories always have a happy ending. They predict that God by way of some emissary or influence will eventually release the oppressed and repressed feminine in our world to make its unique contribution toward a better, more candid, playful yet profoundly serious society and Church. The late Dorothy Parker already provides evidence of this in that polite yet caustic poem she once addressed to the condescending men folk in her life:

> In youth, it was a way I had
> > To do my best to please,
> And change, with every passing lad,
> > To suit his theories.
>
> But now I know the things I know,
> > And do the things I do;
> And if you do not like me so,
> > To hell, my love, with you![33]

FOURTEENTH SUNDAY IN ORDINARY TIME

Mark 6:1–6, Frank Baum

Isn't This the Carpenter's Son?

When Toto accidentally knocked over the screen behind which the Wizard of Oz was concealed and Dorothy and her friends discovered him to be nothing other than a little old man, they were very disappointed. Dorothy cried:

> "Are you not a great Wizard?" . . .
> "Not a bit of it, my dear; I'm just a common man."
> "You're more than that," said the Scarecrow, in a grieved tone; "you're a humbug!". . .
> "But this is terrible," said the Tin Woodman; "how shall I ever get my heart?"
> "Or I my courage?" asked the Lion.
> "Or I my brains?" wailed the Scarecrow . . . .[34]

Like human beings down through the ages, Dorothy and her friends believed their own inadequacies could be compensated for only by some all-powerful being who dwelled on some celestial pedestal or in some Emerald City. Dorothy anticipated that her savior, the Wizard of Oz, should appear as an enormous, suspended Head who would say in a deep, deep voice: "I am Oz, the Great and Terrible." That would have been proper. The Cowardly Lion expected Oz to be a ball of fire. In other words, they expected power to appear powerful, extraordinary, marvelous. When they finally realized the Wizard of Oz was only a ventriloquist from Omaha, they lost all hope of redemption. He was just like them: a nobody, a nothing, in no way exceptional. You can imagine them saying, "What shall we do now?"

The citizens of Nazareth felt a similar resentment. They expected their messiah to be someone magnificent, arriving amid clouds of majesty. They didn't expect him to be the kid next door. "Wasn't this Jesus, a local construction worker?" they said. "Isn't he a relative of James and Simon and the mailman? Doesn't his uncle spend most of his time down at the local pub? He's much too ordinary to be a divine emissary." So by their insistence that God be forever awesome, they missed out on the actual presence of the divine in their midst.

What underlies such persistence? Perhaps it's our low self-esteem. Because as long as we insist upon ourselves being empty, inadequate, powerless, brainless, timid—like Dorothy and her friends—we remain free to delegate all creativity, all power to some outside force, to unload all responsibility for the solution of our problems and the redemption of our world on some enormous "other." In other words, God—kept high upon a pedestal—becomes a convenient excuse for our doing nothing. It gives us a legitimate reason for complaining, "Gee, what can I do? I'm only human, not divine."

Perhaps we need someone like Toto to upset our illusions about God, to make us aware that God can be present in an ordinary person from Nazareth, present even in our ordinary selves. Isn't that what the Wizard of Oz, once unmasked, revealed to Dorothy and her friends? Didn't he ultimately make them aware that all the things they craved for—wisdom, heart, courage, "home"—lay somehow within them, ready to shine resplendently out of their own eyes?

And didn't Jesus say, "The Kingdom of heaven is within you"? Didn't he often wonder why we keep coming to Jacob's Well to fill our "empty" buckets, when in fact God resides within us like a wellspring wanting to erupt? And was not Dorothy (who had traveled so far to find her wizard on a pedestal) throughout that very journey wearing those silver shoes? Had she not from the very beginning been standing on a foundation of power that could have gotten her home with three clicks of her heels? And are not we ourselves, contrary to whatever anyone thinks, potentially the poetic presence of God within our families and neighborhood even as Jesus was throughout all those years in Nazareth?

FIFTEENTH SUNDAY IN ORDINARY TIME

Amos 7:12–15, Mark 6:7–13

Thank You, Colman, Wherever You Are

Father Colman Gallacher was a ruddy Scotsman, a Graymoor Franciscan who flourished in the 1950s and 60s. He was a belated vocation, having worked until he was about 35 in the shipyards of Glasgow, and he had a thick, musical Scottish brogue that he could modulate depending on the audience. But more than anything else, he was a dynamic fellow, what we might call a ham, a real showman.

Even as a seminarian he was extrovert enough to make contact with every Scottish Catholic in Boston, New York, Philadelphia, Detroit, Toronto, and places in between to form what he named the St. Margaret of Scotland Guild, which is how I came to know him. Ostensibly, it existed to fund his seminary education and Graymoor projects, but beyond that it became a vital social organization held together by Colman's charisma. Given the size of the Guild, Colman was allowed by his seminary superiors to be present at its many conventions. Upon his arrival at any railroad station in the aforementioned cities, it was like the entry of Christ into Jerusalem. Off the train he would stride, dressed in his Franciscan robes and sandals, tall, resembling in many ways Monty Python's John Cleese. While bagpipes skirled he would extend both hands to greet the throngs of adoring Guild ladies and shout proletarian jests at the equally admiring men folk.

All such conventions began with a Mass in the local cathedral or downtown church and here's where I first witnessed Colman's capacity to ham it up. Remember, he was still a seminarian and could only serve Mass as an acolyte but—I'm telling you!—his slow, stately transfer of the missal from one side of the altar to the other, his equally solemn way of pouring water from the cruet, his genuflections! Sir Laurence Olivier could not have upstaged the celebrant any better! You can only imagine what his performance must have been like once he was indeed ordained and could celebrate his own Mass.

Well, the reason I'm telling you about Colman is that he was also a great speaker, full of anecdotes told in that delicious brogue. And so I influenced a recently ordained priest to have Colman preach at his first Mass. And I'll never forget the simple story he told in his very elaborate way. He caught the congregation's attention at once by mentioning the First World War. It seems there was a company of Scottish soldiers that had ventured too far out into No Man's Land (as one might expect of Scotsmen) and were soon isolated from their own trenches. Nor could they indicate where they were or call for help, because their single portable phone line was cut. As their casualties grew and the enemy crept closer to their perimeter, the captain sent back volunteers to find support. Hours went by, darkness fell and no help came. There was only silence, except for the boom and chatter of the guns.

Finally an older sergeant offered to try to trace the broken phone wire and splice it, if he could. Permission was given and out of his foxhole he crawled off into the night and flash of the shells. Minutes went by, a half hour, and suddenly the precious phone came alive. The captain was able to call for covering fire and the company made it back to safety. But as they did, they came upon the old sergeant lying dead in a shell hole, the two broken ends of the wire pinched between his stiffening fingers.

I'll never forget that story and the manly way Colman told it. The moral? According to the Gospel of Colman Gallacher, that's what every priest must do, even at the cost of his life: splice the split between God and us. That's what Christ did on the cross, that's what the prophet Amos attempted to do at Bethel, that's what the Twelve in today's Gospel were commissioned to do, and that's what every Eucharist is all about: reviving contact with the very source of our being lest we remain forever lost in No Man's Land.

SIXTEENTH SUNDAY IN ORDINARY TIME

Jeremiah 23: 1-6

High Sierra: A Rebirth of Images

Not long ago I spent a weekend walking in the high Sierra meadows around Carson Pass and above Squaw Valley. Mid-July is the time of year when so many of the mountain wildflowers blossom in clusters among the rocks and along the margins of the lakes. Tiny splashes of scarlet, lavender, white, yellow, pink, blue, purple, and flaming orange. There aren't enough words for color in the English language to describe every hue of larkspur, mountain geranium, Sierra shooting star and other minute blossoms scattered across the landscape.

All of this reminded me of a friend's dream. He was a retired priest whose career came to a close just when Vatican II changed the rubrics of the Eucharist and its language from Latin to the vernacular. Thereafter he was plagued for a long time with a recurring nightmare in which he was celebrating Mass and, before an increasingly restless audience, stood bewildered by the new rubrics to the point of paralysis, very much like a case of "mike fright." He once confided all this to me and noted how one of these dreams was especially memorable. Here again he found himself presiding at the Eucharist, standing at the high altar of a dark cathedral facing a vast congregation gathered out beyond the sanctuary and the same paralysis came over him. He wasn't sure what words to say, what page to turn to, what gestures to make. He just froze.

Then as he looked down at the missal on his left he noticed that it was the old Latin Mass after all, the one with which he was so familiar. It was open to the canon, the core element of the Mass, the initial Latin words of which were *Te igitur, clementissime Pater.* And, with great relief, he thought, "Hey, I can do this!" Then suddenly every letter on the page changed into a flower, row upon row of violets, daisies, lupines, primroses, and clover. With his hands extended in a gesture of prayer, he froze again! "What do I do?" he whispered to the young priest standing at his side. The young priest quite calmly replied, "Read what it says."

We are heirs to a religious tradition that began with colorful, dynamic stories of Adam and Eve, Cain and Abel, Abraham and Sara, of Jacob's wrestling with an angel, of little Moses hidden in the bulrushes. We are heirs to the tragedy of Saul, the passion of David and Bathsheba, the poetry of the psalms, and the metaphors of the prophets, all of which have profoundly influenced so much of the great literature of the West. We are heirs to the Gospel parables, anecdotes of healing and forgiveness, accounts of human transfiguration and resurrection. In other words, we are heirs to a religious tradition whose narratives and images offer us a profound understanding of our human condition and ever so gradual access to fullness of life.

And it was in this meadow God wished us to graze, and yet I suppose it was inevitable that down through centuries this tradition would undergo rational analysis and become distilled, translated into handy formulae and codes of conduct so abstract and impersonal that many believers have long since gone off seeking something more relevant to their needs in exotic religions, crystal gazing or fundamentalist enthusiasm.

"Woe to the shepherds who mislead and scatter the flock of my pasture," says the Lord in today's first reading. But then we also hear a divine promise: "Behold, I myself will gather the remnant of my flock . . . and bring them back to their meadow; there they shall increase and multiply."

We live at a time when God fulfills this promise. My friend's dream of a page of black print changing into a garden of delight could have been no merely personal revelation but a sign of the times. As a millennium so grievously tormented by ecclesiastical, political, and economic strife has come to a close, have we not been summoned by the Holy Spirit (notably during Vatican II) to start "reading the flowers" again, to probe all the stories and images of our biblical lore (and indeed the whole literature of our culture through which they resonate) and thereby once more acquire color, fragrance, a mystical and ethical radiance as individuals and a Church?

SEVENTEENTH SUNDAY IN ORDINARY TIME

2 Kings 4:42–44, John 6:1–15, Kenneth Grahame

Seeing beyond Appearances

The sibling children of Kenneth Grahame's *The Golden Age,* ranging in age from six to eleven, had lived among the adults of their household long enough to acquire a critical attitude toward them all. As the narrator says:

> These elders . . . having absolute licence to indulge in the pleasures of life . . . could get no good of it. . . . They might dabble in the pond all day, hunt the chickens, climb trees . . . yet they never did any one of these things.
>
> On the whole, the existence of these Olympians seemed to be entirely void of interests, even as their movements were confined and slow, and their habits stereotyped and senseless. To anything but appearances they were blind. For them the orchard (a place elf-haunted, wonderful!) simply produced so many apples and cherries or it didn't . . . . They were unaware of Indians, nor recked they

anything of bisons or of pirates (with pistols!), though the whole place swarmed with such portents.[35]

Needless to say then, when told that an uncle just returned from India was about to visit their home, they jumped to critical conclusions. They had met other uncles as inadequate as the adults they lived with. For example, "there was Uncle Thomas—a failure from the first . . . his rooted conviction seemed to be that the reason of a child's existence was to serve as a butt for senseless adult jokes . . . ." And then there was the younger Uncle George, who at first showed some promise, allowing the children to introduce him to their pets, until he met their governess Miss Smedley, from which moment on "Uncle George's manner at once underwent a complete and contemptible change."

Their expectations of this new Uncle William were therefore low. Throughout the course of his stay they couldn't quite make up their minds about him, but in the end (after he had departed for the train station accompanied under orders by their younger sibling Harold) the rest of the children were about to rate him negatively, when Harold returned and stood speechless before them. Then "slowly drawing his hand from the pocket of his knickerbockers, he displayed on a dirty palm one-two-three-four half-crowns!" "Buy what you like [Uncle William had said]—make little beasts of yourselves—only don't tell the old people, mind!" Dreamily, little Charlotte said, "I didn't know that there were such good men any-where in the world. I hope he'll die to-night, for then he'll go straight to heaven!"

All of this seems to show it's not wise to fall into a per-sistently critical attitude toward everything and everyone. People and reality may surprise us if we can get over this habit we acquire so early in life of never giving them the benefit of the doubt. An author much appreciated by my wife says that when Jesus (as he did last Sunday) looked with compassion upon the crowds around him, it doesn't mean he looked upon them with piteous condescension but that he saw in them so many possibilities for good and longed to see them realized. He longed to see them become the prolific miracle each could be. In other words, he saw more than meets the usually critical or passive eye we all possess—even as Elisha and Jesus in today's readings saw more than a few loaves and fishes but ample resources to feed a hundred (even 5,000) souls.

One of the most difficult things confronting me in this extremely negative age of scapegoatism in which we live is to pass from a critical to a Christic (that is, merciful, hopeful, affirmative, joyful, constructive) perception of people and reality. How important it is that I do so—if only to avoid the fate of our story's repentant Selina, who "bewailed herself with tears and sobs, refusing to be comforted; for that in her haste she had called this white-souled relative a beast."

EIGHTEENTH SUNDAY IN ORDINARY TIME

Exodus 16:2–4, 12–15, Emily Dickinson

Praestet Fides Supplementum Sensuum Defectui

Today we read about how, when the Israelites were starving in the desert, God sent them quail and manna. Last week we heard of how Elisha fed a hundred people with only 20 barley loaves and of how Jesus did him one better by feeding 5,000 with five loaves and two dried fish.

Next week we'll read of how, when Elijah lay down weary in the desert, he woke up to find a hearth cake and jug of water by his head, placed there by an angel, and how he walked sustained by that food 40 days and 40 nights to Mount Horeb. A week later we'll read in the book of Proverbs of Lady Wisdom, who dresses her meat and mixes her wine and sends out invitations inscribed: "To him who lacks understanding, I say: Come, eat of my food and drink the wine I have mixed."

With the harvest season coming upon us, these readings about nourishment seem very appropriate. And, of course, their obvious message is that we are all on a long and often difficult journey through life (through what the Lectionary calls Ordinary Time) and need more than material fare to survive. We need spiritual nourishment if we are ever to reach the Promised Land of true maturity. But that message being obvious, I'd like to dwell on another aspect of these episodes.

Have you noticed how Elisha's servant saw only 20 barley loaves where Elisha saw enough to feed a hundred people? Or how the disciples saw only five loaves and two fishes where Jesus saw enough to feed 5,000? Or how today where the grumbling Israelites look around and see only desert and famine staring them in the face, Moses foresees a camp covered with quail and a desert covered with fine flakes like frost—manna everywhere! And it was Elisha and Jesus and Moses who had the truer vision. The seemingly "realistic" perception of the others fell short of reality.

What would we have seen, had we been there? Probably only the 20 loaves or the five loaves and two fishes or simply a desert. And why is that? Because we've been conditioned to doubt the possibilities of life. We've been taught to be careful, strategic in our assessment of our environment and other people. Indeed, we have a tendency to deny much of reality, to make things we don't like "vanish." We so often exaggerate our own importance that we cast everything else in shadow.

How can we remedy this blindness? By getting the caution and guilt out of our lives and letting faith, hope, and love manage our senses. Then, like Jesus, Elisha, Moses, Rembrandt, Shakespeare, and every saint and artist, we will see reality as a banquet spread before us, a multitude of nutritious experiences—nothing to be excluded, not even the spinach, not even the seemingly distasteful and indigestible people and events we encounter. Remember what

God said to Peter when he refused to taste the non-kosher things God let down on that magic table cloth in Joppa: "Rise, Peter, take and eat; it is not for you to call profane what will in fact nurture you into becoming a whole, profound, nutritious human being yourself."

It's hard, of course, for us to acquire the vision Elisha, Jesus, and Moses shared, to see much where there is apparently little. But if we keep at it, a beautiful and bountiful world, a world of multiple dimensions may emerge out of the barren landscape that confronts us—at least by the time we die. What is it Emily Dickinson says?

> I've seen a Dying Eye
> Run round and round a Room—
> In search of Something—as it seemed—
> Then Cloudier become—
> And then—obscure with Fog—
> And then—be soldered down
> Without disclosing what it be
> 'Twere blessed to have seen.[36]

NINETEENTH SUNDAY IN ORDINARY TIME

1 Kings 19:4–8, Herman Melville

God's Way of Weaning Us from Whine

Today's first reading tells of the ninth-century BC prophet Elijah, who alone had the courage to confront that wicked Israelite king, Ahab. Mindful of that biblical king, when Herman Melville wrote his classic story *Moby Dick*, he chose to call the obsessed captain of the *Pequod* by the same name, Ahab. And when the story's hero Ishmael and his friend are about to embark on Ahab's whaling venture into the Pacific, it's a shabby looking fellow named Elijah who says, "Shipmates, have ye shipped in that ship? . . . Names down on the papers? . . . some sailors or other must go with him, I suppose; . . . God pity 'em!"[37]

Melville's Captain Ahab is a symbol of someone we know very well. He is an angry man. Having lost a leg to that mysterious whale called Moby Dick, he is determined to get even. But there's more to it than that. To him the whale is but the mask of a whole universe that seems intent on messing up his life. He resents this universe and whoever is behind it. He would control it, subject it to his demands, and bring to bear all his technological power to eliminate its mystery, its elusiveness.

In the process, he loses whatever tenderness he once possessed. Family, crew, his ship—all of them become expendable in his quest to win, to settle to his satisfaction what he defines as the "problem" of human existence. "Swerve me? ye cannot swerve me," he cries. "The path to my fixed purpose is laid with iron rails, where-on my soul is grooved to run." Needless to say, Ahab is not a happy man nor will he ever be, because he views everything in terms of his hurts and vindication.

There are times, however, when he is offered a chance to nourish his soul on better fare—experiences meant to enkindle whatever embers pulsate within his bosom. As when, looking out on an ocean sunset that made the warm waves blush like wine, he thinks, "Oh! time was, when as the sunrise nobly spurred me, so the sunset soothed." Or as when, remembering his wife and child back in Nantucket, he cries out to his mate Starbuck: "I feel deadly faint . . . as though I were Adam, staggering beneath the piled centuries. . . . Close! stand close to me, Starbuck; let me look into a human eye." Or as when Captain Gardiner of the *Rachel* comes on board to plead with Ahab to delay his quest for Moby Dick and join him in his search for his sons (one but 12 years old), adrift he knows not where. "For God's sake—I beg, I conjure. . . . Do to me as you would have me do to you in like case." But every time Ahab hardens his heart. He resists every opportunity offered him to come out of his vindictive trance, to embrace and allow himself to be embraced.

Do we find something of ourselves in Ahab's behavior? Do we, too, feel at times so vindictive that we see nothing in every direction but a menacing sea or (as in the case of Elijah himself in today's reading) a barren desert? And yet both Melville and the Bible remind us that God bombards us with so many invitations to snap out of such depression.

Sunrise, sunset—what are they and all the wonders of nature but sacraments designed to awaken us to God's presence among us? A child's bruise, a friend's divorce, a wooden cross and fresh flowers set up along a local highway—are they not equivalent to Captain Gardiner's plea to Ahab? Are they not equivalent to a hearth cake and jug of water placed by an angel beside depressed Elijah's head? Are they not divine interventions designed to nurture our capacity to weep instead of whine, to care instead of rage and thereby arrive at Mount Horeb—symbolic of the bigness of God?

TWENTIETH SUNDAY IN ORDINARY TIME

Proverbs 9:1–6, John 6:51–58, David Schickler

Pill's Mystery Ingredient

Ever since Jesus changed water into wine at Cana and nourished 5,000 followers with but a few loaves and fishes, our civilization seems compelled to invent sequels to these miraculous events—in stories like *Babette's Feast* and more recently in David Schickler's "Wes Amerigo's Giant Fear" published in *The New Yorker*. Wes' fear was losing his livelihood. A chef and caterer, he had just taken out a third mortgage on his home to maintain his wife Helen and their three children, the youngest being Pill, who was seven years old and who loved to pray. They often found her kneeling somewhere with her eyes closed.

Of course, there was some hope. The Harkness-Ives wedding party was booked for the coming weekend and 200 swordfish steaks awaited Wes' magic touch. But he still kept having nightmares, which woke up the whole family. He could give no rational explanation for his apprehension. To maintain some composure he'd resort to reciting a catalogue of everything he was sure of: his age, his occupation, and so on. Such behavior worried his wife and older children but not Pill. Balanced on the back of her Irish Wolfhound, she simply looked into her father's eyes, placed two fingers over his mouth and told him not to worry.

Nevertheless, the night before the Saturday wedding he bolted out of bed again. Sensing something strange he shook his wife at two in the morning and told her to follow him. Down they went to the kitchen and there they found Pill covered with flour and surrounded by forty bread pans filled with uncooked dough seasoned with spices of every kind. When Wes demanded what she was doing, she told him that he would see.

The next day, Wes, Helen, and the two older children were at work setting up the reception hall for the wedding banquet. The guests would soon be on their way and all Wes had to do was bring in and prepare the 200 swordfish steaks stored in his van. And what did he find? His daughter Pill sitting beside a vat of sticky maraschino juice in which she had immersed not only every swordfish steak but also every one of 200 truffle cakes! All he could think about was how he was ruined, and how he would have nothing to feed those people. But Pill giggled and pointed to the van's shelves where she had stacked all those bread pans she had filled with dough the night before. She told him he could cook those.

In the dining room, the newlyweds and the guests awaited their Swordfish Cilantro. What they got—much to their dismay— were baked loaves of every odd shape and flavor, yet as they nibbled away, their initial anger gave way to cries of delight. Pill's bread seemed possessed of every pleasant taste imaginable. The next day (Sunday) the whole town gathered around the Amerigo threshold hungry to know where Pill got her recipe. She told them that it came from the part of her "that floats," a phrase Pill knew to be her mother's definition of one's soul.

Over the past few weeks of the liturgical year, the Lectionary has been regaling us with similar stories of miraculous nourishment: of the 20 loaves Elisha used to feed 100 people, of the manna sent by God to the Israelites, of the hearth cake that sustained Elijah all the way to Mount Horeb, of the five loaves and two fishes Jesus used to feed the crowd. And in today's Gospel we hear Jesus declare himself to be our Bread of Life—himself a mixture of substance and rapture designed to nourish that part of you and me "that floats." What an extended opportunity for all of us to ponder the Eucharist that consciously or unconsciously continues to influence even the imagination of *The* (sophisticated) *New Yorker.*

TWENTIETH SUNDAY IN ORDINARY TIME
TOPICAL: PROVERBIAL WISDOM

The Book of Proverbs, Dorothy Parker

Come, Eat of My Bread and Drink the Wine I Have Mixed

Today's first reading is taken from the book of Proverbs. The proverb was the principal method by which the youth of biblical times were taught how to live ethically and successfully. Written educational materials were hard to come by in the days before the printing press and so pupils were required to memorize brief and often rhymed maxims recited by their instructors—and thereby build up a handy store of wisdom by which they might navigate their way through the challenges of family, business, social, and political life. The book of Proverbs offers hundreds of such pithy sayings used in schools such as perhaps even Jesus attended as a boy. Scholars tell us many go back to the days of King Solomon. Here's a sample:[38]

• The simpleton believes everything but the shrewd man measures his steps.

• Better a dish of herbs where love is than a fatted ox and hatred with it.

• A patient man is better than a warrior, and he who rules his temper, than he who takes a city.

• Pleasing words are a honeycomb, sweet to the taste and healthful to the body.

• Even a fool, if he keeps silent, is considered wise; if he closes his lips, intelligent.

• Like an infected tooth . . . is dependence on a faithless man in time of trouble.

• Like a glazed finish on earthenware are smooth lips with a wicked heart.

• Like a man who seizes a dog by the ears is he who meddles in a quarrel not his own.

Notice how this proverbial method of teaching wastes no time in abstract speculation; rather, it offers the student practical insights drawn from generations of human experience. It deals with the "how" of living rather than theological questions like whether God exists—simply because it takes God for granted, convinced that "only a fool will say there is no God."

Of course anyone who has heard of *Poor Richard's Almanac* and Benjamin Franklin knows that proverbial wisdom influenced even the generations that founded our American republic, offering us ever-valid advice such as the following:

• Diligence is the mother of good luck.

• One today is worth two tomorrow.

• Love your enemies for they tell you your faults.

• Beware of little expenses for a small leak will sink a great ship.

• Anger is never without reason but seldom a good one.

Given the fact that only males were formally educated in biblical times, you will occasionally find proverbs that take a swat at the feminine. Here's one example: "It is better to dwell in a corner of the housetop than in a roomy house with a quarrelsome woman." But these rare put downs have been more than compensated for by our own twentieth-century Dorothy Parker who honed a few cautionary epigrams of her own regarding modern romance and male fidelity. Here are a couple of examples:

> By the time you swear you're his,
> Shivering and sighing,
> And he vows his passion is
> Infinite, undying—
> Lady, make a note of this:
> One of you is lying.

And:

> Oh, life is a glorious cycle of song,
> A medley of extemporanea;
> And love is a thing that can never go wrong;
> And I am Marie of Roumania.[39]

THE ASSUMPTION OF THE BLESSED VIRGIN MARY

Revelation 11:19a; 12:1–6a, 10ab

The Woman Clothed with the Sun

Of all the contents of the New Testament, the letters of Saint Paul to the Corinthians, Galatians, and Romans (among others) are the earliest. In them, Paul mentions Mary, the mother of Jesus, only once, in Galatians: "When the time was right, God sent forth his son, born of a woman." That's it! Paul seems to have known nothing about her, nor does he appear curious. Christ occupied his whole attention.

Then about 64 AD, the Gospel of Mark appeared and here Mary again gets short notice. In one episode, Jesus is teaching in a crowded room and someone says, "Your mother and brothers are outside asking for you." Looking about the room, Jesus says, "Who are my mother and brothers? Here are my mother and brothers and sisters, all you wonderful people." Mary's left to stand outside. And that's all Mark has to say about her.

Then later in the first century along comes Matthew's Gospel with two whole chapters on the birth of Jesus! Surely Mary will get some notice here; a mother's got to be central to a birth story. But no, it's Joseph to whom the angel comes telling him to wed Mary, to flee into Egypt, to return to Nazareth. Joseph, the Magi, and Herod turn the story into a masculine monopoly. Mary has a bit part at best.

About the same time as Matthew's, Luke's Gospel appeared, also with two chapters on the birth of Jesus. But here Mary finally emerges as the central character. This time the angel comes to Mary, who then visits Elizabeth, who greets her with a blessing. Mary then sings her Magnificat. It's Mary to whom the aged Simeon speaks at the Temple. It's Mary who ponders all these events in her heart. It's Joseph who has the bit part.

So how come Luke describes Mary (after hardly any notice over a 50-year period) as key to the arrival of God's grace and presence in this world? Well, Luke may have been alert to the fact that women had always played a key role in Israel's history. At first glance, the Old Testament may look like a book about men operating within a man's world, but a closer look reveals that at almost every critical moment in biblical history a daring, imaginative woman saves the day. There's Rebecca diverting Isaac's blessing from Esau to Jacob. There's Pharaoh's daughter saving Moses from infanticide. There's Naomi and Ruth compelling a reluctant Boaz to marry Ruth, without which union there would have been no David and Solomon. There's Thamar, Rahab, Deborah, Judith, and Esther, each equivalent to an early Joan of Arc. In every case, the men folk are fatalistic; it's the women who have the imagination to perpetuate life.

Luke tells a similar story. Zachary the priest is the embodiment of the male leadership of Israel caught up in habitual, ritual behavior that has become sterile. Along comes an angel promising an age of miracles and Zachary says, "I need to think about this," and then he becomes mute instead of poetic. So off flies Gabriel to a woman quite ready to say yes to the absurd, to release the music humanity has repressed for too long.

From hardly any notice at all, woman's prominent role in the redemption of the world finally gets recognition—as it did again (for those who have eyes to see) in the 1950 proclamation of Mary's bodily assumption into heaven—to take her place on the pedestal next to Christ. And ever since then, women have become ever more visible and influential in our world, even within our once exclusively male sanctuaries and professional theological associations. Where will it end! Hopefully in song, in a revival of grace and imagination within our sometimes-prosaic institutions. Let a new millennium begin!

TWENTY-FIRST SUNDAY IN ORDINARY TIME

John 6:60–69, Samuel Beckett

Expectation

Estragon:	Let's go.
Vladimir:	We can't.
Estragon:	Why not?
Vladimir:	We're waiting for Godot . . .
Estragon:	And if he doesn't come?
Vladimir:	We'll come back to-morrow.
Estragon:	And then the day after to-morrow.
Vladimir:	Possibly.[40]

Estragon and Vladimir are two middle-aged men who, in Samuel Beckett's play *Waiting for Godot* seem to have spent every day of their lives by a rural roadside waiting for this character Godot to arrive.

We human beings have ever tried to make sense of who we are and what this world is all about. To that end we have produced great myths, philosophical systems, and scientific theories to explain it all. And for many people, one or another of such explanations may satisfy. But not Beckett. Like current postmodern theorists, Beckett wonders whether all our myths and theories may simply amount to games we play to deceive ourselves.

The fact is that (from Beckett's point of view) we don't know where we came from, nor what value a life can have that must end in death. And yet, erase all our discredited explanations, we still keep waiting for Godot. We retain within us this perpetual expectation for some meaningful answer, which expectation compels even Beckett to keep writing, to keep probing , despite his skepticism.

Throughout the play Vladimir and Estragon waver between hope and despair and otherwise behave the way we all do during this interval between birth and death. They eat, they argue, they get involved in long discussions about discrepancies in the Bible. They focus (as scientists do) on specific objects like a shoe, a tree. When a passing blind man collapses in front of them, they discuss endlessly what they should do about it (the way Congress endlessly discusses whether or not people should be guaranteed health care). Vladimir concludes by saying, "Let us do something, while we have the chance! It is not everyday that we are needed . . . . Let us represent worthily for once the foul brood to which a cruel fate consigned us!" Mutual compassion and assistance are at least a wholesome way to pass the time!

But then there is this boy who twice arrives from off stage to keep their hopes alive. He always comes with a message from Godot, never very elaborate but simply: "Mr. Godot told me to tell you he won't come this evening but surely tomorrow." And so as the sun sets for the billionth time, they and the human race wait. They may want really to go, to leave this planetary stage they're on, to say to hell with this crazy waiting game called life. Indeed, the play's dialogue ends with Vladimir saying, "Well? Shall we go? " To which Estragon replies, "Yes, let's go." But as the final curtain falls, the stage directions say, "They do not move." Expectation remains a perpetual human obsession.

As believers we think otherwise. We consider expectation to be the very capacity that makes us human, hopeful, and our hopes haven't been disappointed, for in Christ we have experienced that ultimate messenger from God who is God himself!—a messenger to whom, if he were to ask, "Do you, too, want to go?" I would simply have to reply, "Lord, to whom shall I go? You have the words of eternal life."

TWENTY-SECOND SUNDAY IN ORDINARY TIME

Mark 7:1–8, 14–15, 21–23, Charles Dickens

You've Got to Have Heart

> Father, you have trained me from my cradle? . . . I curse the
> hour in which I was born to such a destiny . . . . How could
> you give me life, and take from me all the inappreciable things
> that raise it from the state of conscious death? Where are the
> graces of my soul? Where are the sentiments of my heart?
> What have you done, oh, Father, with the garden that should
> have bloomed once, in this great wilderness here?[41]

And with that she struck her breast.

So spoke young Louisa to her stern father, Mr. Gradgrind,
in Dickens's novel *Hard Times*. And Mr. Gradgrind deserved to be
spoken to in those terms, for he had been a strict advocate of fact
over fantasy. He ran his household the way he ran his school, whose
policy was "to teach these boys and girls nothing but Facts," to
eradicate all sentimentality and imagination, to make the heart
subservient to the calculating brain for profit's sake. In this way he
might be called a latter-day scribe such as we meet in today's Gospel
reading who valued every letter of the law (the way Gradgrind
worshipped facts), forgetting that the law exists to serve humanity
and not vice versa, forgetting that humane concern for the well-
being of the community and not regimentation should be the aim
and motivation of all law.

The very ambiance of Gradgrind's school reflected something of the hollowness of the man himself and the culture he
would create: a plain, bare, monotonous vault of a place. His mouth
was thin and hard set, his voice inflexible and dry, his carriage
obstinate. His square coat, square knees, square shoulders all served
to emphasize his resistance to the least glimmer of romantic fantasy.

As he stared at the children before him with galvanizing effect from deep set eyes,

> he seemed a kind of cannon loaded to the muzzle with facts, and prepared to blow them clean out of the regions of childhood at one discharge.

Dickens saw in Mr. Gradgrind and the other movers and shakers of his novel, like Mr. Bounderby and Mr. McChoakumchild, symbols of the increasingly heartless, empirical environment in which he lived. Of course, what goes around comes around. Eliminate all pathos from human society; ridicule all faith as foolish illusion and all "bleeding hearts" as wimps and the moment may arrive when people like Mr. Gradgrind may regret their hardnosed, utilitarian philosophy.

Indeed, later in the story, when Gradgrind has to plead with Bitzer, one of his former pupils who is in a position to save his son from prison, he gets the cold shoulder. "Bitzer, have you a heart?" he asks. And the old pupil responds in the properly factual way he had been taught: "The circulation, sir, couldn't be carried on without one. No man, sir, acquainted with the facts established by Harvey relating to the circulation of the blood can doubt that I have a heart." In other words, "we all have pumps, Mr. Gradgrind. Isn't that what you taught us?"

It's almost as though, in their need to avoid all pain or the inconvenient demands of love, people like Gradgrind as well as the scribes in today's reading have put on armor, become like the Tin Woodman in *The Wizard of Oz*, whom the Wicked Witch of the East transformed from a caring young man of flesh and blood into something hollow, metallic and rusty enough for his limbs to resonate with a sound much like the name Gradgrind.

But it's really impossible to eradicate one's heart, no matter how hard one may try. The Tin Woodman found that out and so did Mr. Gradgrind. The rebuke of his daughter quoted at the top of this essay finally awakened him to the dreadful nature of his blindly "factual, empirical" approach to life. And so by the end of the novel we find our author describing Gragrind contemplating his future and asking:

> Did he see himself, a white-haired decrepit man, bending his hitherto inflexible theories to appointed circumstances; making his facts and figures subservient to Faith, Hope and Charity; and no longer trying to grind that Heavenly trio in his dusty little mills?

I'm sure he did.

TWENTY-SECOND SUNDAY IN ORDINARY TIME
TOPICAL: LITURGICAL TIME

Philippa Pearce

Thirteen O'clock

In her really profound "children's" story *Tom's Midnight Garden*, Philippa Pearce describes young Tom Long as upset when told he had to stay with city relatives until his brother got over the measles. It meant living with a stern uncle and aunt who rented a flat from a widowed landlady who lived in the attic of her converted old house. Tom hoped the place had at least a back yard where he might play outside. But no way! He was told the yard was fenced, paved and full of dustbins.

　　Tom was still awake that night when the downstairs clock struck 13! Thirteen o'clock? Tom went downstairs to investigate. The clock showed the usual 12 hours. Why had it struck 13? He then noticed the door to the backyard. He opened it and saw not a concrete pen filled with dustbins but a garden beyond which lay meadows and a distant river. His uncle must have been teasing him.

The next morning Tom ran downstairs to explore his new-found garden. But opening the backdoor in daylight, he saw only the smelly yard his uncle had described. What was going on? Perplexed, he lay awake that night until the clock struck 13 again. Down he went and, sure enough, at that mystic moment there again he saw that garden! This time he saw some boys and a girl named Hatty, but only Hatty seemed to see Tom. She winked at him and eventually as he returned to the garden night after night, they became close friends. Tom learned that she was an orphan who lived with an abusive aunt and cousins. He became her confidant and she welcomed the consolation he brought her night after night—even as he delighted in her company. Often they went on excursions to the distant river and even to a town and cathedral beyond the meadows.

When Tom's parents eventually sent for him to return home, he didn't want to leave. He decided on his final night to return to Hatty and her midnight garden and stay forever. Down he went, opened the back door, and groped in the dark only to feel dustbins all about him. The garden was gone. "Hatty! Hatty!" he cried out, waking all the tenants in the building.

The next day, as Tom packed, his aunt worried about the impact of last night's commotion on the landlady upstairs. Tom offered to go up and apologize. He found the widow quite shaken. "I've come to say I'm sorry," said Tom. "Your name's Tom isn't it?" she said. "You called out . . . . Oh, Tom, don't you understand? You called me: I'm Hatty."[42] For weeks, old Mrs. Bartholomew been dreaming of her troubled childhood days spent in the garden that once blossomed behind her house and somehow Tom had stepped right into her childhood. Somehow he had become capable of passing from ordinary clock time into that thirteenth hour where he could walk with that young Hatty of long ago.

Tom's aunt was impatiently waiting for Tom to come downstairs to return home. And so he had to say, " 'Good-bye, Mrs. Bartholomew,' shaking her hands with stiff politeness; 'and thank you very much for having me.' " But as he reached the foot of the stairs, "he turned impulsively and ran up again—two at a time—to where Hatty Bartholomew still stood . . . ." Later his aunt told her husband that "he ran up to her, and they hugged each other as if they had known each other for years and years, instead of only having met for the first time this morning. There was something else, too . . . . Of course, Mrs. Bartholomew's such a shrunken little old woman . . . but, you know, he put his arms right round her and he hugged her good-bye as if she were a little girl."

The clock strikes 13 for us every time we attend the Eucharist because Church time is a time that's not confined to whatever year or millennium we're actually in. People of faith know that at every Eucharist Christ's Last Supper of long ago is once again made present to us, as is that heavenly banquet around whose table all our dead are even now gathered with the risen Christ. It's quite an assembly and it's eternal. I know the bulletin says we have Masses at 7:30, 8:45, and so on, but they're really all scheduled for 13 o'clock!

TWENTY-THIRD SUNDAY IN ORDINARY TIME

Isaiah 35:4–7, James 2:1–5, Mark 7:31–37, Eudora Welty

Campfire Girl

Among Eudora Welty's stories is one called "A Visit of Charity." It's about a 14-year-old Campfire Girl named Marian, who, dressed in a red coat and white cap and bearing a potted plant, pays a visit to an Old Ladies Home on a wintry day. The place itself, made of white-washed brick and reflecting "the winter sunlight like a block of ice," must have added to the chill.[43] The nurse who opened the door was also dressed in white.

"I'm a Campfire Girl," said Marian. "I have to pay a visit to some old lady." The visit was worth three points (toward a merit badge?), which will prove to have been the only motivation Marian had to visit the place. The nurse asked if she were acquainted with any specific residents. "With any old ladies?" stammered Marian. "No—that is, any of them will do." The nurse took her down a corridor to one of the rooms and knocked, saying, "There are two in each room." "Two what?" asked Marian as the nurse pushed her through the open door. Suddenly Marian was alone with two old women.

One was feeble but up and about. She wore "a terrible, square smile . . . on her bony face." With a claw-like hand she plucked off Marian's hat. "Did you come to be our little girl for awhile?" she asked, and then she snatched the potted plant. The other woman was lying flat in bed, irritable. "Stinkweeds," she said, referring to the plant. And so it went, with the one being cloyingly sweet and the other increasingly cranky over every remark her roommate made. The tension in the room made Marian go rigid.

The irritable bedridden women summoned Marian to her side. "Come here!" Marian trembled. (The other woman explained the situation: "She's mad because it's her birthday.") "It is not my birthday," screamed the woman in bed. "No one knows when that is but myself and will you please be quiet . . . or I'll go straight out of my mind!" Marian "wondered about her . . . for a moment as though there was nothing else in the world to wonder about." It was the first time she had ever experienced anything like this. Then the old face in the pillow slowly collapsed. "Soft whimpers came out of the small open mouth . . . she sounded like—a little lamb." Surprised and embarrassed, Marian turned to the other woman and said, "She's crying!"

And with that she jumped up, grabbed her cap and, eluding the other lady's grasp, ran from the room, down the hall, past the nurse and out into the cold air. "Wait for me!" she shouted to a passing bus and jumped on, then sat down and took a bite of an apple she had hidden for herself.

Saint James lectures us today on discrimination. Even back in the early Church some Christians preferred the company of pleasant folk to the apparently shabby ones. I myself visit a nursing home almost every day where I have an aged relative and I must admit, I bridle at the thought because of the condition of so many of its residents—and the forecast I'm given of my own inevitable physical and mental deterioration. Saint James tells us to get over that; that a treasure awaits us at the margins of polite society— a treasure Marian almost discovered when she said, "She's crying."

And what is that treasure? An awakening of our closed minds, of our muted senses and consequently of our hearts, of a sense of solidarity with people in pain, indeed an awareness of our own pain, the loss of that numbness we characterize as equilibrium. In other words, an awakening of our humanity! Marian didn't stay long enough to fully experience such an awakening, but hopefully one day she'll return to that Old Ladies Home with something more than a merit badge in mind.

TWENTY-FOURTH SUNDAY IN ORDINARY TIME

Isaiah 50:4–9, Mark 8:27–35, John Henry Newman

So Must the Son of Man Be Lifted Up

We're familiar with those scenes from Dracula where all the hero has to do is hold up a cross and Dracula wilts away. The rising sun has the same effect on the Count, who can only operate when all is dark.

Well, don't laugh but, as a Church, we are about to pull out that trusty cross again. And why? To help us deal with the encroaching darkness of fall and winter or rather all that it symbolizes. Spring is a distant memory. Summer with its ever-brighter mornings and long evenings is almost over. The autumn equinox is upon us—that time of the year when night returns to claim an equal share of our time and will begin in fact to dominate our days, making them shorter, colder, and even depressing.

Our tradition realizes, of course, that these longer nights and shorter days are the consequence of a natural process occasioned by the tilt of the earth and its rotation around the sun. But why let an opportunity for spiritual support go unused? And so our tradition asks us to imagine spring and summer as symbolic of those brighter aspects of our lives—of youth, faith, romance, energy, joy, success, vitality. But what about those other experiences that cast a shadow—the aging process, sickness, mortality, failure, mistakes, depression? Sooner or later these too must be encountered like the shadows of autumn and winter—to assault our faith, diminish our hope and possibly even our capacity for love. That being the case, what better time than now with the onset of autumn for the Church to pull off its Count Dracula trick and raise up the cross to confront the approaching seasons of darkness?

And how does she do that? By way of today's readings that remind us of the Crucifixion of Jesus and by way of the feast of the Triumph of the Holy Cross, strategically situated on September 14 of every year just before the autumn equinox. This festival initially commemorated Saint Helen's reputed discovery of the true cross in 320 AD and its later recovery from Persian invaders in 629 AD. But on a symbolic level listen to the Gospel selection (John 12:31 ff.) that used to be read at this autumn festival in which we hear Jesus saying to us: "Now the ruler of this world will be driven out. And when I am lifted up from the earth, I will draw everyone to myself . . . . The light will be among you only a little while. Walk while you have the light, so that darkness may not overcome you. Whoever walks in the dark does not know where he is going. While you have the light, believe in the light, so that you may become children of light."[44]

In other words, whenever you find yourself entering some season of darkness in your life (whether it coincide with the onset of autumn or winter or not), keep your eyes fixed on the cross of Christ, which like a beacon must always signal the inevitability of a Transfiguration, a Resurrection, a rebirth of light, yes,

Christmas!—the victory of unquenchable hope and love over the Prince of Darkness, despondency and despair that has as its culmination the Resurrection.

And as a little mantra to recite as autumn darkness now sets in, why not fall back on that old favorite by John Henry Newman, which he composed during a critical period in his life:

> Lead, kindly Light, amid the encircling gloom,
> > Lead thou me on!
> The night is dark, and I am far from home—
> > Lead thou me on!
> Keep thou my feet; I do not ask to see
> The distant scene—one step enough for me . . . .
>
> So long Thy power hath blest me, sure it still
> > Will lead me on,
> O'er moor and fen, o'er crag and torrent, till
> > The night is gone;
> And with the morn those angel faces smile
> Which I have loved long since, and lost awhile.[45]

TWENTY-FIFTH SUNDAY IN ORDINARY TIME

Mark 9:30–37, William Wordsworth

He Took a Little Child

William Wordsworth shared Jesus' appreciation of childhood as expressed in today's Gospel reading. In his poem with that long title, "Ode: Intimations of Immortality from Recollections of Early Childhood," Wordsworth says that a child, but freshly born, retains a closer connection than we weary adults do to the realm of God

from which we came. He recalls how his own powers of perception
were so fresh when as a boy,

> . . . meadow, grove, and stream,
> The earth, and every common sight,
> To me did seem
> Apparelled in celestial light . . . .[46]

Such experiences convinced him that that so fresh a soul
had to come from afar:

> Not in entire forgetfulness,
> And not in utter nakedness,
> But trailing clouds of glory do we come
> From God, who is our home . . . .

But kids soon learn the ways, worries, prejudices, and
polarizations of the adult world. "Heaven lies about us in our
infancy!" says the poet, but

> Shades of the prison-house begin to close
> Upon the growing Boy . . . .

By the time we're six years old we find ourselves practicing
the roles and situations that await us as adults—roles and
situations displayed before us by our parents.

> See, where mid work of his own hand he lies . . . .
> See, at his feet, some little plan or chart,
> Some fragment from his dream of human life,
> A wedding or a festival,
> A mourning or a funeral . . . .
> Then will he fit his tongue
> To dialogues of business, love or strife . . . .
> Filling from time to time his 'humorous stage'
> With all the Persons, down to palsied Age,
> That Life brings with her in her Equipage . . . .

And so up we grow to adopt the adult code of survival until

It is not now as it hath been of yore;—
      Turn whereso'er I may,
        By night or day,
The things which I have seen I now can see no more.

       The Rainbow comes and goes,
        And lovely is the Rose . . . .
     The sunshine is a glorious birth;
     But yet I know, where'er I go,
That there hath passed away a glory from the earth.

Such was the condition of Jesus' disciples in today's Gospel reading. For them, life (even in the company of Jesus!) had become a hassle of ambition, competition, confrontation, the promotion of one's own ego over that of others. But rather than reason with them, what does Jesus do? He places a child in their midst and says, "Try to recover something of the wonder, the openness, the playfulness you once knew and enjoyed as children. Loosen up, smile, slow down, let go and let God. Trust!" And he might add, "Stop going through your day like someone in a trance, too preoccupied to see what's in front of you. Focus. Self is not something you preserve; it's something you discover by wholeheartedly engaging with this sacramental moment, this person, this sunset, this starling, this ritual— as so many gateways to a deeper experience of reality and God."

Certainly Wordsworth found in his observation and remembrance of the qualities of childhood something helpful to his sanity as he went on to remark:

        O joy! that in our embers,
        Is something that doth live,
        That nature yet remembers . . . .

    . . . those first affections,
    Those shadowy recollections,

Which neither listnessness, nor mad endeavor . . . .

Nor all that is at enmity with joy,

Can utterly abolish or destroy!

      Hence in a season of calm weather,

          Though inland far we be,

Our souls have sight of that immortal sea

          Which brought us hither;

      Can in a moment travel thither,

And see the Children sport upon the shore,

And hear the mighty waters rolling evermore.

TWENTY-SIXTH SUNDAY IN ORDINARY TIME

Mark 9:38–43, 45, 47–48, Herman Melville

Lead with a Heart

Captain Ahab made his living killing whales. He sailed the oceans of the world with one commercial intent: to turn these magnificent creatures of God into oil to light the homes and businesses of human beings before the days of gas and electricity. Once a whale was harpooned and brought alongside the ship, every crewman became a butcher. Suspended out over the whale, they would slice into its body with sharp spades (even as sharks chomped away from below). A hook would then be lowered and long strips of the skin (called blubber) would be lifted on board and boiled down to yield in some cases a hundred barrels of oil.

But by the time we meet Captain Ahab in Herman Melville's story *Moby Dick*, he has other intentions in mind as he sets sail from his homeport on the doomed ship, the *Pequod*. For he now walks on an ivory leg and bears a scar left on him by the backlash of a huge white whale named Moby Dick that escaped him on a recent voyage. "Threading its way out from among his grey hairs, and continuing right down one side of his tawny scorched face and neck, till it disappeared in his clothing, you saw a slender rod-like mark, lividly whitish."[47] It looked like the seam lightning might make on the trunk of a great tree.

Since that incident, commerce has been no longer his primary intent in going to sea. Now it's vengeance. He has become obsessed with that white whale and all the contradictions and ambiguities of life that it represents—and he's out to conquer it, to get even. His first mate tries to suggest a more profitable course for the *Pequod* than Ahab's futile pursuit of Moby Dick. "What will the owners say, Sir?" he asks, to which Ahab responds, "Let the owners stand on Nantucket beach and outyell the Typhoons. What cares Ahab?"

Of course, it's not long before he communicates his obsession to his crew:

> Aye . . . my hearties . . . it was Moby Dick that dismasted me; Moby Dick that brought me to this dead stump I stand on now . . . and I'll chase him round Good Hope, and round the Horn, and round the Norway Maelstrom, and round perdition's flames . . . till he spouts black blood and rolls fin out.

Well, we all know what happened. Such obsession, such inability to let go of bitterness, a self-righteous need for "vindication" leads to the destruction of the *Pequod* and Captain Ahab and all his crew, save one. It's this same kind of obsession that possessed France after its defeat by Germany in 1870, resulting in World War I—and possessed Germany after 1918, producing World War II. It's the same kind of obsession manifest in our political and international headlines every day and on a smaller scale in controversies that divide families, neighborhoods, a Church.

This may have been one of the things Jesus had in mind in today's Gospel when he says in metaphorical but no uncertain terms: "If you can't let go of a grievance, cut off your hand; if your foot's stuck in some insoluble argument, cut it off; if your eye insists on remaining jaundiced over some offences, pluck it out." In other words, let go of the things that have begun to obsess you, before you wake up someday to find yourself in garbage up to your neck (Gehenna was Jerusalem's city dump).

Obsession and vindictiveness are not Christ's way. Christ's way is tolerance, openness to the possibility that the Holy Spirit is operative even in the "other camp." His way is trust, hope, dialogue, respect, and communion. His way is the way of a woman I knew who, whatever the competitive card game might be, always led— on principle—with a heart.

TWENTY-SEVENTH SUNDAY IN ORDINARY TIME

Hebrews 2:9–11, Isak Dinesen

How Flora Gordon Became a Flower Garden

> The Lady Flora was by no means ugly . . . she was a giantess . . . . Wherever she went, she stood head and shoulders above the men with whom she conversed. She was correspondingly vast of hips and chest. Her hands and feet, in themselves beautiful, were of a size to match those marble angels in my own chapel . . . . Nose, jaw, ears and bosom, as well, in this lady were of goddess-like dimensions . . . she carried herself exceedingly straight and high. Her attire was . . . never embellished. . . . Her only jewels were a single row of pearls . . . . She also declined to follow the British custom of shaking hands in meeting and parting.[48]

Thus Cardinal Salviati describes the Scottish heiress Flora Gordon in Isak Dinesen's story "The Cardinal's Third Tale," contained in her collection *Last Tales*. She had a *noli me tangere* ("don't touch me") way about her. Her favorite author was

Jonathan Swift, who is noted for his "strange and terrible loathing of the earth and of humanity as a whole." In a word, she was a purist, a puritan—disgusted or at best amused by everything she encountered in this world.

To indulge her cynicism, she condescended to visit Italy, where she met an untidy Franciscan named Father Jacopo. She delighted in scandalizing him with her disdain for Catholicism, which she thought a much too earthy religion. Father Jacopo found her overwhelming. To him she seemed to view reality from some high pillar far beyond his reach—"straight and colossal, never giddy, one with the marble on which she stood." He tried to console himself with the thought that perched so high, perhaps God might reach her if his earthbound priest couldn't. But no! "From her altitude," he mused, "she would glance down at the men and women round the pillar's foot, confirmed in her conviction of their pin-size."

Christianity is about the Incarnation of God (as noted in today's second reading), the belief that God became flesh, became human in Christ. Some early Christians found that belief repugnant. Their preference was to keep God high on a pedestal, untainted by creaturely limitations. Ah, but the question is: whom did they really want to keep on a pedestal? God or themselves? Because, after all, aren't we all a bit like Flora Gordon? Don't we all imagine ourselves a bit above and beyond it all, unlike "all those other people"—born aristocrats able to target and bemoan the imperfections of the world around or, should I say, below us? It's a human tendency called pride by some, recoil by others.

So no wonder many recoiled from the idea that God could come down and join the crowd. What a terrible precedent! For then we would all be required to come down off our own pedestals. There would be incarnations all over the place! We'd have to give up our elevated judgment seats, our fascination with penthouses, and become human. We'd have to identify with people, get our hands dirty, bleed for others—like Christ, of whom Saint Paul said, "Though he was in the form of God, he did not count equality with

God a thing to be clung to, but emptied himself, taking the form of a servant, being born in the likeness of humanity—obedient unto death, even death on a cross." The Incarnation turns our world upside down by reminding us that the way down is really the way up.

Father Jacopo finally did get Flora Gordon off her pedestal. He took her into St. Peter's Basilica, where—first of all—she couldn't help but realize how tiny she was! By the story's end we find her at a convalescent resort for people with venereal disease. (It seems Isak Dinesen has her pick it up indirectly when compelled to imitate another pilgrim and kiss the bronze foot of Saint Peter's statue in the Basilica!) "Alas," says the cardinal, "her full clear harmonious voice of former days was gone. But in her present broken, low and hoarse voice, like to the cackle of an old wise raven or a cockatoo, there was a new joviality, a mirthful forbearance with and benevolence toward the frailty of humanity."

TWENTY-EIGHTH SUNDAY IN ORDINARY TIME

Wisdom 7:7–11, Evelyn Waugh

Wisdom

What is wisdom? It means more than being smart. I've known smart people who were in no way wise. And I've known illiterate people who were oracles of wisdom. One was my Italian grandmother whom my Aunt Lena described as "dumb-smart"—in other words, a person who in any gathering might appear somewhat "out of it" but was quietly wise to everything that was going on. My grandmother knew precisely where she was in the universe—something that can't be said of so many pundits who worry over who we are, where we are in space and time, what's it all about—and produce inconclusive and expensive books on the subject. My grandmother could have answered all those questions convincingly in a few words, if she thought they required asking in the first place.

So what was it she had? Intuition? Some sixth sense? Obviously it's something more than intelligence. It's something that wells up from the gut, the heart, so that people who refuse to allow feeling to contaminate their thought processes are not likely to be very wise. And I would caution one about taking their advice based solely on their impressive credentials. Go to my grandmother instead. She might not be able to answer all your questions but she'd quickly sort out the ones that really mattered.

There's a scene in Waugh's *Brideshead Revisited* about an aristocratic Catholic family in Britain that illustrates what I'm trying to say. Toward the end of the novel, the widowed Lord Marchmain has returned to his estate to die. Cara, his Italian mistress, has accompanied him and now Cara and Marchmain's grown children, Brideshead, Julia, and Cordelia, have gathered to discuss when it would be prudent to call for a priest to anoint the bedridden, semi-conscious father. They're concerned that it might startle Lord Marchmain, who had become a very strong-willed apostate, and cause a scene.

Charles Ryder, Julia's agnostic fiancé, is present. To him their discussion seems inane. He proposes they leave the poor man alone. But no, on they go, arguing just when would be the best opportunity, until Charles impatiently says, "I wish someone would explain to me quite what the significance of these sacraments is."[49]

His request creates no little confusion. The family had never before been asked to explain things like the Anointing of the Sick. They slip into a conflicting exchange of pious opinions: "I think my nurse told me . . . ." "You've got it all wrong, Cara." "Well, I remember when Alphonse de Grenet died, Madame de Grenet had a priest hidden outside the door . . . ." "Well, she was wrong." "I never heard that before." Charles is not impressed. Obviously they have no clear or communicable idea on why a priest must be called. Why won't they just let the man die in peace? His logic reduces them to silence. "There was a pause in which Julia sighed and Brideshead drew breath as though to start further subdividing the propositions."

Then "in the silence Cara said, 'All I know is that *I* shall take very good care to have a priest.' 'Bless you,' said Cordelia. 'I believe that's the best answer.'" Cara's gut, her heart has spoken and wins delightful Cordelia's spontaneous confirmation. Wisdom has spoken out of a logic Charles Ryder could not presently fathom but would begin to ponder when later, a priest having been called, he beheld the comatose Lord Marchmain himself slowly raise his hand to his forehead, breast, and shoulders in response to the priest's request for a sign of faith.

Saint Augustine says there were two trees in paradise, the tree of knowledge (or science) and the tree of life (or wisdom). Some people in our day and age would eat only of the tree of knowledge. People of faith feed also off the tree of life, whose roots draw nourishment from depths far more primeval and true.

TWENTY-NINTH SUNDAY IN ORDINARY TIME

Mark 10:35–45, James Thurber

Daydreams

Driving his wife to the hairdresser, Walter Mitty drifted into a fantasy. He was commander of an eight engine navy seaplane. A winter storm raged all around him. His crew was nervous. But not Mitty. Determined to go on, he revved the plane up, compelling his crew to beam with admiration at his indomitable will.

Only when Mrs. Mitty complained he was driving too fast did Mitty snap out of his daydream. But no sooner did he drop her off than, passing a hospital en route to a parking lot, he now fancied himself a famous surgeon. The patient was a millionaire and friend of the president. He was suffering of obstreosis of the ductal tract. The anesthetizing machine had broken down. No one knew how to fix it. Mitty did. Then the worried specialists pleaded with Mitty to take over the operation, which he did with his usual nonchalance—until he almost hit a Buick and suddenly had to return to the real world.

James Thurber's story "The Secret Life of Walter Mitty" is all about this fellow who transcends his prosaic life by imagining himself a hero, admirably perfect in every way. In other words, he's a character just like you and me. I have lived a good deal of my own life in a dream world. Bombarded as we are by larger than life figures in films and history books, how can we help but aspire to similar prominence and glory? My boyhood fantasy was to be a cowboy like Ken Maynard or like swashbuckling Errol Flynn. Or I might ponder myself as a comrade of Jimmy Cagney in "The Fighting Sixty-ninth," heroically charging a German trench, or as a movie tenor or baritone like Alan Jones or Nelson Eddy serenading a starry eyed soprano, or as Spencer Tracy playing Father Flanagan or Pat O'Brien as Father Duffy. This latter fantasy propelled me into a seminary at the age of 15!

We're all subject to such reveries: to be a celebrity, excel in school, win the lottery, become governor of California—to transcend our anonymity, be possessed of all the answers, *perfect.* Where does this dream of perfection come from? Our tradition seems to trace it to the kiss God gave Adam in Eden. Touched by God, we have ever since aspired to be more than chemistry and biology will allow. But we seem to have mistaken the full intent of that divine kiss. What we seem to have savored most was the flavor of God's omnipotence, so that ever since Eden we have become addicted to power, builders of one imperial Tower of Babel after another—and on a lesser level, dreamers like Walter Mitty or like James and John in today's Gospel, imagining ourselves as superior in one way or another.

When all the while, the intent of God's kiss in Eden (as Jesus has informed us) was to share with us a taste of his mercy, to make us creatively merciful toward ourselves and others and all things great and small, to make us persons, not potentates. And think about it. Do we impose perfectionism on our kids? I like mine just as they are! They were beautiful to me from the moment I first saw them helpless and incontinent in a bassinet. Their quirks endear them to me. Their mistakes make me love them all the more. Then why can't we be as merciful to the face we see in the mirror? Why can't we value our own selves as God made us? If it weren't for our flaws, we'd all be like mannequins in a store window.

Walter Mitty, leaning against a drug store wall, has a final fantasy. He imagines himself a patriot about to be executed. He refuses a blindfold, takes one long drag on a cigarette and snaps it away—the way any solitary film hero would do before a firing squad. This makes me think. In concluding his story in this way, maybe Thurber is offering us a suggestion of just how we might (figuratively speaking) get rid of this perfectionist in our bonnet: ready, aim, fire!

TWENTY-NINTH SUNDAY IN ORDINARY TIME
TOPICAL: THAT PERSONAL TOUCH KNOWN AS GRACE

Harper Lee

Hey, Mr. Cunningham, How's Your Entailment Gettin' Along?

It was night in the small 1930s town of Maycomb, Alabama. Atticus Finch sat on a chair in front of the town jail. As lawyer for Tom Robinson, a young African American accused (falsely) of assault, he had taken up his post because he expected a lynch mob to show up. His daughter Scout and her brother Jem noticed his late absence from home and decided to see what was going on. They reached the town square and saw Atticus alone, reading a newspaper while night bugs danced in the light around his head. The children also noticed four cars driving round the square—to stop in front of the jail. Scout and Jem ran to observe things from nearby. Men began to emerge from the cars. As Harper Lee writes in her story *To Kill a Mockingbird* how they move ominously toward the jail door.

They warned Atticus to stand aside. Tension mounted. Atticus would not move. The men felt challenged. Suddenly Scout ran to be by her father and Jem followed. Atticus told them to go home. The children wouldn't budge. Someone from among the lynch mob growled, "You got fifteen seconds to get 'em outa here." Scout sized up the men and noticed the familiar face of Mr. Cunningham.

Mr. Cunningham was a poor farmer who to save his farm during the Depression had mortgaged and entailed himself beyond any hope of solvency. Atticus provided him legal representation gratis and Cunningham would repay him with a sack of hickory nuts or a load of stove wood. Scout had often befriended his barefoot son at school. Scout now called out to him, asked him how his entailments were doing, reminded him that she was Jean Louise Finch, a schoolmate of his son Walter and of what a nice boy he was and of how Walter once had dinner at her house and of how she once got the better of him in a fight but they remained good friends. And finally she asked Mr. Cunningham to say "hey" to Walter for her.

Atticus and the men stood with their mouths half-open. Then Mr. Cunningham underwent a change. He squatted down and took Scout by both shoulders and said, "I'll tell him you said hey, little lady." He then stood up and said he'd tell Walter "hey" for her. He then stood up and led the lynch mob back to their cars and off into the night. What had Scout done to defuse that potentially lethal confrontation? She got personal. She didn't see the mob. She saw someone with whom she felt a personal tie and appealed to that, thereby compelling Mr. Cunningham to extricate himself from the impersonal abstraction he had become—from the inflexible "principles" he had allowed to petrify his behavior, neutralize all that was benign within him. She brought out in him his paternity—his humanity—and this "virus" began to spread. Feeling began to compete with the mob's thirst for vengeance.

The world in many ways would make of us automatons, driven by abstract ideologies or grievances. Christ came to make us realize that we are *persons,* to help us see beyond the "principles" of scribes (who always seem so ready to stone someone to death). He came to introduce into human relationships that personal touch otherwise known as grace—the kind of personal touch God would apply to you and me, if we would let him. And wherever a vestige of personality remains within the most hardened of hearts, may not a graciousness even there be revived?

THIRTIETH SUNDAY IN ORDINARY TIME

Mark 10:46–52, Lewis Carroll

Myopia

Alice had been foolish to follow that rabbit down his rabbit hole, for now she found herself in a realm where none of her usual standards applied. First she found herself falling, but in slow motion for ever so long a time and without mortal consequences. Then she found herself one moment very small, and another moment very tall. Which was she?

Next she kept meeting all these animals that talked with an air of superiority that reversed her notion of the hierarchy of being (human, superior; all else inferior). Here Alice was treated as a quite ignorant person who had the poor taste to speak fondly of her cat to a mouse. She was so caught up in her own narrow, human way of looking at things she assumed that was the only way. She became terrified. "Dear, dear! How queer everything is today! And yesterday things went on just as usual. I wonder if I've changed in the night? Let me think: *was* I the same when I got up this morning? . . . But

if I'm not the same, the next question is, 'Who in the world am I?' "[50]
In her desperation to impose her "normality" on her surroundings
she tried reciting the multiplication table but it came out wrong;
her old arithmetic was no longer valid.

Then she tried reciting a disciplinary poem of Isaac Watts
the English children were taught in school:

> How doth the little busy bee
>> Improve each shining hour,
> And gather honey all the day
>> From every opening flower! . . .

> In books, or work, or healthful play,
>> Let my first years be passed,
> That I may give for every day
>> Some good account at last.

But it all came out wrong:

> How doth the little crocodile
>> Improve his shining tail,
> And pour the waters of the Nile
>> On every golden scale!

> How cheerfully he seems to grin,
>> How neatly spreads his claws,
> And welcomes little fishes in,
>> With gently smiling jaws!

And that's exactly how Alice felt, as if she were being swallowed up by some strange new world so different from the Victorian
world she knew. But ultimately she had no reason to be afraid, for
what she was experiencing was her transition from the narrow frame
of reference within which she had been taught to view reality. She
was being invited to see the limitations of her assumptions about life

and reality, invited to expand, discover instead of constrain people and things to conform to her acquired set of labels (like that empty jar she passed while falling down the rabbit hole which was nevertheless labeled "ORANGE MARMALADE"). It's the same thing Jesus does throughout the Gospels—to the blind Bartimaeus in today's Gospel from Mark, to the man born blind in John's Gospel, to the two disciples on the road to Emmaus in Luke's Gospel.

The latter were trapped within their own inherited, rigid expectation regarding the Messiah and his mission (it had to be political). They, too, were possessed of the normal and fatalistic notion that crucifixion meant defeat and a dead man was simply dead. Until Jesus, in effect, said, "What little sense you have! Reality is so much deeper, loaded with so many more possibilities than your language and arithmetic and assumptions will allow!" And then he fractured a loaf of bread before their eyes to symbolize how they, too, must experience the fracture of their biased evaluation of things and open up to realities, to adventures beyond their present ken.

And it says, "With that their eyes were opened . . . whereupon he vanished from their sight." Even as the rabbit and the Cheshire Cat vanish in Wonderland, but only to entice us further along the path of faith to ever heightened awareness and fullness of life.

THIRTY-FIRST SUNDAY IN ORDINARY TIME

Mark 12:28–34

Linnie Never Failed

Our neighbor Linnie died in mid-January. She was 96 years old, sound of body and mind right up to the end. She lived alone— or, as she would say, independently. She was a true descendant of pioneer stock. She married a man much older than she and consequently became the instantaneous mother of seven stepchildren. That didn't prevent her from also raising four of her own. Nor did it spare her the grief, given her longevity, of outliving most of them.

When her husband died in 1959 she was still a vigorous 52 years old, young and beautiful enough to remarry. Instead, she decided to set back the clock and behave like a woman with her whole life ahead of her. She went to college. Sonoma State University had just opened its doors and Linnie was enrolled in its first class of freshmen. Consequently she became a member of the first class to graduate from Sonoma State—and what's more, insofar as she was placed at the head of the line, she became the *first person* to graduate from that increasingly eminent institution. And now at the age of 55 she began a career as an elementary school teacher whose pupils remember her to this day.

By the time we met her as new neighbors 25 years ago she was a 71-year-old retiree—but a very active one, cultivating an organic garden, keeping us posted on the happenings of the neighborhood, teaching the Bible, and otherwise assisting in the guidance of the local Baptist church.

Naturally, we were there for her memorial service, where I was personally so moved by the minister's simple eulogy. He began by highlighting the events of Linnie's life and career. And then he recited that famous passage from Saint Paul's first letter to the Corinthians:

> Love is patient; love is kind. It is not jealous or boastful; it is not arrogant or rude. Love does not insist on its own way; it is not irritable or resentful; it does not rejoice at wrong but delights in the truth. Love bears all things, believes all things, hopes all things, endures all things. Love never fails.

Now listening to the rhythmic recitation of that somewhat abstract passage one's mind might wander, even as our minds so often do wander during familiar biblical readings. But as if he were developing a latent image on film into a magically visible positive, the minister recited the passage again, replacing the word love with Linnie's name—and, my, how those words came to life:

> Linnie was patient; Linnie was kind. Linnie was not jealous or boastful; Linnie was not arrogant or rude. Linnie did not insist on her own way; she was not irritable or resentful; Linnie did not rejoice at wrong but delighted in the truth. Linnie bore all things, believed all things, hoped all things, endured all things. Linnie never failed.

The Gospel of John says that with the arrival of Jesus "the Word became Flesh and dwelled among us." What that Baptist eulogist was saying to all of us is that Saint Paul's words became flesh in our neighbor Linnie—that the commandment recited by Jesus in today's Gospel reading ceased to be an abstraction to anyone who knew her.

I don't know about you but from now on I'm going to keep that preacher's text from Saint Paul in front of me daily and hope that by my reformed behavior I may begin to see my own name emerge on the page as the legitimate subject of all those sentences that begin with love.

THIRTY-SECOND SUNDAY IN ORDINARY TIME

Mark 12:38–44, George Eliot

"Them"

One September when my wife and I entered the twelfth-century cathedral of Ravello (a terraced town overlooking the Mediterranean south of Naples), we were struck by the beauty of its tall white walls and timbered ceiling and especially by the high pulpit, which stood to the right of the central aisle. The pulpit's sculpted stone was inlaid with gold mosaics woven around a colorful mosaic of the Madonna, and its six spiral legs rested on the backs of six prowling marble lions.

But what gave us immediate pause were the strains of Schubert's *Panis Angelicus* sung by a soprano voice coming from behind the front pillars of the nave. I thought it was a tape played for the benefit of visitors, but it was nothing so commercial. Advancing toward the main altar, we discovered it to be the voice of a young woman practicing for a festival. We then turned to view a side altar and were startled to see a middle-aged woman in a flowery skirt standing on a ledge of the altar, dusting the gold lattice work below a Renaissance painting. What with her colorful skirt it was difficult at first to distinguish her from all the other ornaments—until she smiled and waved her dust rag.

Such delightful experiences were not unusual, for in Italy Jane and I were left continually astounded by one such cathedral or chapel after another, fresh with flowers, loaded with aesthetic expressions of faith dating from the Middle Ages and the Renaissance. And then there were the museums! And I had to think: when we study the history of the Church during those centuries, all we read about are continual conflict between the Popes and German emperors, controversies over discipline, one Pope living in Avignon and another in Italy, holy wars against heretics and Turks. We read about the Borgias, Colonnas, and Medicis seeking the papacy by hook or by crook, and about a not so Innocent VIII and Alexander VI and about Pope Julius II decked out in armor to resist the armies of the king of France—all of which contributed to the Reformation, which left Europe broken and bleeding right down into the twentieth century. And you have to ask yourself: under such administration, how in heaven's name did the Church survive!

Then you look at these gems, these sanctuaries with their fresh flowers and tenderly set mosaics and ruby windows and frescos and interior domes so painted with clouds and sky and an ascending Christ that you almost conclude there's no dome at all. It's a veritable glimpse of heaven. And you hear that soprano voice and you see that woman in her colorful skirt dusting away and you realize that this is why the Church survived! Not because of its politics but because of these sacramental chambers in which the invincible faith of its men, women, and creative visionaries has remained so wonderfully evident and alive.

Regarding that woman on the altar dusting away, she reminded me a bit of Dolly Winthrop in *Silas Marner*. Nowhere in the Gospel will you hear Jesus say, "Thou art Dolly and upon this Rock I will build my Church." And yet it's those matriarchal Dolly's of our past to whom we owe so much, who brought a despairing Silas Marner Christmas cakes with I.H.S. imprinted on them, assuring him that "whativer the letters are, they've a good meaning,"[51] and who assured him that if he were to get to church

> and see the holly and the yew, and hear the anthim, and then take the sacramen', you'd be a deal the better, and you'd know which end you stood on, and you could put your trust i' Them as knows better nor we do . . . .

She always referred to God as "Them," which in its blend of intimacy and reverence must have pleased God more than all the highfalutin titles given him by philosophers and theologians.

THIRTY-THIRD SUNDAY IN ORDINARY TIME

Mark 13:24–32, Evelyn Waugh

He Will Dispatch His Messengers and Assemble His Chosen

On her first journey from Britain to the continent of Europe, Saint Helena was disturbed by the long wall that ran along the Rhine River, separating the territory of the Roman Empire from the uncivilized tribes and wild forests of Germany. So (in Evelyn Waugh's novel *Helena*) she asks her husband, the Emperor Constantius (whom she had married in Britain), "Must there always be a wall?"

Constantius was amused by her dismay. "I love the wall," he said.

> Think of it, mile upon mile, from snow to desert, a single great girdle around the civilized world; inside, peace, decency, the law, the altars of the gods, industry, the arts, order; outside, wild beasts and savages, forests and swamp, bloody mumbo-jumbo, men like wolf-packs; and along the wall the armed might of the Empire, sleepless, holding the line. Doesn't it make you see what the City means?[52]

According to the Bible, it means narrow-mindedness! According to the Bible, Cain, who slew the nomad Abel, was the first to build a city, to put up fences, palisades to insulate him against influences he could not comprehend and control. Control was what he and subsequent walled empires wanted, totalitarian control over people and any other variables in life that might threaten their security. And that's why the Bible delights in tales about cities like Jericho, whose walls came tumbling down at the mere sound of liturgical music—because walled civilizations and closed gates are symptomatic of closed minds and hearts, of an insecurity that can become aggressive and lethal if we don't watch out.

Nevertheless, we still remain partial to walls. Fatalists in Europe and the Balkans or Middle East have preferred them to any intermingling of the ideological differences or ethnic groups that dwell there. And no sooner did the Cold War end with its variety of cinder block, barbed wire, and electronic walls than we have found people wanting to build walls along our own border, despite the fact that God will not tolerate such enclosure any more than he could tolerate being boxed up himself in that Holy of Holies in Jerusalem and, therefore, one day blew the place wide-open. When a nation's (or Church's!) trust, curiosity, creative imagination, and courage begin to fail, it begins to talk of walls, closure, isolation, exclusion, all of which adds up to suffocation, a deadly "normality."

Perhaps that's what disturbed Saint Helena about that interminable Roman wall that her husband so admired. "What d'you mean, must there always be a wall?" he says. And she replies:

> Nothing; only sometime I wonder won't Rome ever go beyond the wall? into the wild lands? Beyond the Germans, beyond the Ethiopians, beyond the Picts, perhaps beyond the ocean there may be more people and still more . . . I meant couldn't the wall be at the limits of the world and all men, civilized and barbarian, have share in the City?

What City might that be that is in no way exclusionary but inclusive, that does not discriminate, that is a multicultural playground made up of people like my nephew and nieces who are already Irish, Italian, Polish, and Lithuanian—Joseph's coat of many colors, Noah's rainbow—in no way plain, but beautiful? Certainly Helena had more in mind that Constantius' imperial Rome—something more akin to that universal Jerusalem foreseen in the book of Revelation, made up of citizens at long last radiant with mutual grace.

THE COMMEMORATION OF ALL THE FAITHFUL DEPARTED

Romans 6:3–9

Seedling

My mother-in-law Ellen died at about 5 AM on August 24. She was 86 years old. In the autumn of 2001 she suffered a stroke that impaired her mobility, and while she could still speak, she did so rarely. Her features, however, retained their capacity to communicate, recognize people, and react to dialogue. She could still smile.

Nevertheless, it was downhill from there. Ever so gradually she yielded to a permanent need for a wheelchair; her occasional speech gave way to silence. A weariness came over her. Finally she had to be placed in a convalescent hospital. From sitting up, she soon spent every day in bed or a wheeled recliner. Her eyes remained closed except for rare moments when she seemed to stare at no one in particular. Physically, she became a fragile remnant of her former self, and then she breathed forth her spirit. It had been a long decline, frustrating to those who loved her. As for me, it was one more experience of how a once blossoming, accomplished human being—possessed of mind, beauty, interests, and ambitions—can collapse into a pale wraith of its former self.

But here's where our religious tradition, with all of its customs and poetry, came sweeping in like a cloud of angels to retrieve that pitiful remnant of Ellen's life to remind us of her true nature, worth, and durability beyond the ups and downs of biology. For example, tradition required that we hold a wake, that we arrange her in an ornate bed set within a chamber of more or less décor, surrounded by mementos of her life story and flowers tagged with sentiments of friends far and wide. Recognition! Affirmation in the face of death. Celebration of a life.

And then there were the prayers. How thoughtful it is to say the rosary at a wake (after the Liturgy of the Vigil of the Deceased). Of course, we've streamlined it to no more than one or two decades. But what if we actually recited all 15, recalling first the Joyful Mysteries: the birth and childhood of Christ—then the Sorrowful Mysteries, recalling the suffering that awaits us all—but then the Glorious Mysteries of Christ's Resurrection and Ascension and Mary's assumption and coronation! For what are we doing when we thus meditate on the life cycle of Christ and Mary but integrating Ellen's life into that cycle, coaxing Ellen's own past phases of joy and suffering toward a glorious finale equivalent to that of Christ and Mary—a finale that will never end.

And then there were the passages read at Ellen's funeral liturgy, which again like angelic messengers descended to rescue Ellen's life from the tomb—to assert her worth despite the ravages of time—with words from the book of Proverbs:

> Her value is beyond pearls.
> Her husband, entrusting his heart to her, has an
>   unfailing prize . . . .
> She rises while it is still night, and distributes food to her
>   household . . . .
> She enjoys success in her dealings; at night her lamp is
>   undimmed . . . .
> She reaches out her hands to the poor . . . .
> She is clothed with strength and dignity, and she laughs at the
>   days to come.
> She opens her mouth in wisdom . . . .
> Her children rise up and praise her; her husband, too, extols her.
> Many are the women of proven worth, but you have excelled
> them all.

And then we heard another angel out of the book of Revelation informing us that for Ellen there shall be no more death for "Behold, I make all things new." And another recalling the words of Jesus regarding Jairus' daughter: "She is not dead, but asleep. Little girl, I say to you, arise." And then again there were all those flowers reminding us that unless the seed die it cannot bear fruit, reminding us that Ellen, reduced physically to a seedling of her former self, was at last ready to blossom in ways—eternally—that we we'll never imagine until we follow her one day through the valley of the shadow of death to lie down ourselves in green pastures—beside still waters.

LAST SUNDAY IN ORDINARY TIME
OUR LORD JESUS CHRIST THE KING

John 18:33b–37

Camelot

In this third millennium, when whatever monarchs exist are little more than figureheads, it seems out of date to close each liturgical year with a feast dedicated to Christ the King. Kings have been long gone ever since Oliver Cromwell decapitated Charles II and the guillotine did the same to Louis XVI and the First World War resulted in the toppling of Kaisers, czars, and every other absolute kingpin. People are no longer impressed by royalty except as an heirloom to be gossiped about. So why—back in 1925—did Pope Pius XI decree this annual festival of Christ as our King?

Well, first of all because he liked the whole idea of feast days, festivals, and celebration! He thought them so much better a medium of instruction than the abstract doctrinal and moral directives we expect from the Vatican. Listen to what he says in his encyclical promulgating the feast of Christ the King: "People are instructed in the truths of faith and brought to appreciate the inner joys of religion far more effectually by the annual celebration of our sacred mysteries than by any official pronouncement of Church teaching. Such pronouncements usually reach only a few and the more learned of the faithful . . . feasts reach them all; the former speak but once, the latter speak every year . . . . The Church's teaching affects the mind primarily; her feasts affect both mind and heart. . . . People are composed of body and soul . . . and need festivals . . . in all their beauty and variety to stimulate them to drink more deeply of the fountain of God's teaching that they may make it a part of *themselves*" (author's emphasis).

So initiating a feast day, an occasion for banners and special events and royal fanfare was in itself a fun thing to do as well as pedagogically smart! And as for this one being about Christ as our true and only King, I wonder if Pius' intent was not unlike that of the producers of that memorable musical *Camelot,* which even to this day awakens in modern audiences a longing for the return of a legendary King Arthur from his island vale of Avalon to reconstitute in our too, too prosaic times his transcendent kingdom of grace and chivalry.

Perhaps that's the spirit in which we ourselves should approach our festival of Christ our King—as a moment to renew our resolve to think regally, to remember that Christ came to make each of us an aristocrat and never to let anyone make us think anything less of ourselves, to be persistently proud of our genealogical link to God Almighty, to be ever ready to exercise our birthright to behave generously, with a noblesse oblige akin to that of Christ. The feast is not so much about doctrine as about an attitude, a way of looking at the world, a courtly life style and continual quest for the Holy Grail—to be attained, of course, at every Eucharist we attend.

In Washington Irving's story of Rip Van Winkle, we have this comical character who wanders into the Catskill Mountains of New York and, after imbibing during a bowling party with some phantom Dutchmen, falls asleep for 20 years. When he awakes the Revolutionary War has been fought and won and a political election preoccupies his village. As he stares "in vacant stupidity" at the rallies and debates, he's asked whether he's a Federal or a Democrat. "Alas! gentlemen," he replies with dismay, "I am a poor and quiet man . . . and a loyal subject of the King, God bless him." Needless to say, he's almost run out of town! But so say I in this world of transient politicians and slogans and perpetual contests of right versus left: "Alas! gentlemen, as to my fundamental allegiance, I am a loyal subject of Christ my King, God bless him."

MEMORIAL DAY

Wilfred Owen

Some Afterthoughts

Not long ago I was excited to discover my great, great granduncle, Henry Wood, was at the Battle of Gettysburg. At age 48 he had joined up with the Ninety-ninth Pennsylvania Infantry as a private. His 14-year-old son, Henry Jr., also joined up—as a fifer. Henry Jr. remained with the regiment from July of 1861 until January of 1863 when he was discharged because (as his records state) "he enlisted as a fifer but he couldn't fife." The older Henry went on to see action with the Third Corps at the Second Battle of Bull Run, Fredericksburg, Chancellorsville, and Gettysburg, where on the second day he fought amid the carnage of Devil's Den and on the next day stood in reserve 50 yards from that famous stone wall, breached momentarily by Pickett's Charge.

Now why should I be excited over that? Why should I value having been somehow present at a great battle by way of a blood relative? Or for that matter, why should I still feel a thrill when I see a rerun of *The Charge of the Light Brigade* or *The Fighting Sixty-ninth,* whose cast seemed to include every member of Hollywood's Irish Mafia: Cagney, McHugh, Hale, O'Brien, Lundigan? I recall as a boy sitting through that latter film three times of an afternoon and then going home, my ears still ringing with the strains of *Garry Owen*. Or why am I still moved every year when someone gives me an artificial red poppy, reminding me of that forgotten poem?

> In Flanders fields the poppies blow
> Between the crosses, row on row . . . .[53]

I am a peaceful person. As a Christian and a rational person, I am opposed to war as a solution to problems. I certainly don't want to see my son go to war. I think war is a waste of life and resources, as any experienced veteran will testify. And yet I can't deny the excitement I feel when confronted by the image of that lad in *The Red Badge of Courage* picking up a tattered flag and shouting, "Come on! Come on!" to his hesitant companions. Is it all a symptom of something barbaric lingering within my otherwise civilized breast?

I like to think it's something else—perhaps envy, the envy people trapped in some comfortable, undemanding routine feel toward the unselfish heroism that so often emerges within the crucible of war, where suddenly individuals exhibit a courage above and beyond the call of duty, stand up to death, exhibit what Lincoln so aptly called that last full measure of devotion.

I like to think that's what moves me when I hear *Garry Owen* and makes me proud to know my great, great granduncle showed up for roll call at Gettysburg. It's not war. War is a waste or, as someone has said, "War is energy enslaved." Literal warfare usurps our nobility, our capacity for heroism, in order to apply it to aims unworthy of it: territorial, economic, ideological, vengeful. When all the while God has planted this nobility within us to fight the good fight, to win the greater battle of building a more humane world by no less heroic, passionate acts of human service, art, eloquence, caring! Why have we allowed war to have such a monopoly on all that's heroic in us when we know it sometimes takes more guts to care about people every day than charge into a cannon's mouth?

So on Memorial Day I thank my great, great granduncle and the men of the Ninety-ninth and those who lie in Flanders fields and Normandy and the Ardennes and the vast Pacific—for an example of a heroism we all need to manifest beyond the confines of war. For in their heart of hearts I know all veterans must agree with Wilfred Owen, who died in combat just a few days before November 11, 1918:

> Out there, we've walked quite friendly up to Death . . . .
> > We chorused when he sang aloft;
> We whistled while he shaved us with his scythe . . . .
>
> > We laughed at him, we leagued with him, old chum . . . .
> > We laughed, knowing that better men would come,
> And greater wars; when each proud fighter brags
> He wars on Death—for lives; not men—for flags.[54]

FATHER'S DAY

Luke 15:1–32

A Father's Dilemma

It seems to me that the older brother in Saint Luke's parable of the prodigal son has a right to be upset. May we not imagine him frequently standing right in front of his father explaining a farm problem or requesting funds for supplies? And does his father pay attention to him? No! His eyes gaze right past the faithful son's ear to focus on some promising speck on the horizon. Indeed, the father's preoccupation with his wayward son may have allowed the whole burden of the estate's management to fall on the elder brother's shoulders, tripling his responsibilities. Of course, it's not that he couldn't handle it. The father must have known him to be dependable—and he was that indeed. But he wouldn't have considered an occasional birthday card or a pat on the back a distraction from his work! After all, he was a son and not a hired hand. He must have expected some attention even though his little brother had long ago learned how to monopolize his daddy's affection.

And now that wayward son has come back and there's all this fuss. The prize calf has been butchered; expensive festivities have begun. And the elder brother is out working in the field—totally uninformed, a forgotten member of the family! No embossed invitations for him! It takes one of the servants to say, "Oh by the way, junior is home." So no wonder the fellow pouts. No wonder the father has to come out and plead with him to join the party!

I ponder this scenario because it brings back memories of how much my own paternal attention was unevenly divided between an older son who has never been a problem and a younger son whose early involvement in drugs preoccupied me over all the years leading up to his death. And there I was engaging with my younger son Philip, ever on his case, ever trying to be there to save, to support but more essentially to assure him of how much I loved him, while my Adam, the older boy, carried his own weight, made wholesome friends, could be counted on when needed, chose a lovely person to marry, is secure and independent to this day. And yet I fear that even now, though my younger boy has passed away, whenever Adam catches me on the rebound, we wind up talking about Phil!

And I begin to think: what indeed is my relationship to Adam, his not having been a problem child but a pure gift from heaven? What can one feel about a child who has always been there behind my shoulder as I've gazed down the road for signs of Phil—and who, if I were to turn and look at him, would shine like a golden boy, possessed of qualities that I've always felt transcend me who am merely his father?

There's a scene in Shakespeare's *King Lear* in which—to receive their inheritance—Lear's three daughters have to verbalize their love for him. Two of them tell him poetically (and insincerely) just what he wants to hear. When he comes to Cordelia she's honestly speechless, for Cordelia's love is too profound for words. This incident perhaps explains the nature of my love for my elder son.

As compensation for my preoccupation with Philip, I could take my cue from Saint Luke's parable and say to Adam, "My son, you have been here with me always and everything I have is yours!" Such a remark should convey sufficient love to relieve him of any impression I've taken him for granted. But, you know, in the end, if I am required to articulate the actual love I feel for the older brother in my own family parable, I'm going to have to fall back on Cordelia's honesty and say, "Dear Adam, please try to fathom the eloquence of my silence in your presence for 'I cannot heave my heart into my mouth.'"

Endnotes

1. William Blake, Letter to Thomas Butts, November 22, 1802, in *The Letters of William Blake,* edited by Geoffrey Keynes (New York: The Macmillan Co., 1950), p. 79.

2. Marcel Proust, *In Search of Lost Time,* vol. 2, translated by C. K. Moncrief and Terence Kilmartin (New York: Random House, The Modern Library paperback edition, 1988), p. 317 ff.

3. Psalm 26 from the Authorized Version of the Old and New Testaments, *The Comprehensive Teachers' Bible* (London and New York: S. Bagster and Sons, Limited, Title: *The Comprehensive Teachers' Bible,* 1907).

4. Betty Smith, *A Tree Grows in Brooklyn.*

5. Lois Lowry, *The Giver* (Boston: Houghton Mifflin Company, 1993), p. 179 f.

6. W. H. Auden, *For the Time Being* (Northampton, England: Faber and Faber Limited, 1945), p. 123.

7. Frank Norris, *McTeague* (Penguin Books, 1982), p. 4. All quotations are from this edition.

8. George Eliot, *Middlemarch,* edited by W. J. Harvey (Harmondsworth: The Penguin Edition English Library, 1965), p. 283 f.

9. Emily Dickinson, *Final Harvest, Emily Dickinson's Poems,* selections and introduction by Thomas H. Johnson (Boston: Little, Brown, and Company, 1961), p. 123. This poem's number in the *Complete Poems of Emily Dickinson* is 501.

10. William Shakespeare, *The Complete Works of Shakespeare,* edited by George Lyman Kittredge (Boston: Ginn and Company, 1936), p. 649.

11. Psalm 136/137 as translated in the Revised Standard Version of the Old Testament.

12. Christina Georgina Rossetti, "De Profundis" in *The Poetical Works of Christina Georgina Rossetti* (London: Macmillan and Co., Ltd., 1914), p. 398.

13. Miguel De Cervantes, *Don Quixote* (New York: Random House, The Modern Library, 1930), pp. 812–815.

14. James Dalessandro, *1906* (San Francisco: Chronicle Books, 2004), pp. 232–233. All quotations are from this edition.

15. William Wordsworth, "Ode (Intimations of Immortality)" in *Wordsworth: Selected Poetry,* edited by Nicholas Roe (New York: Penguin Books U.S.A., Inc., 1992), p. 207.

16. Anne Porter, "Wartime Sunday" in *An Altogether Different Language* (Cambridge, Massachusetts: Zoland Books, 1994), p. 35.

17. Marcel Proust, *Swann's Way,* translated by C. K. Scott Moncrieff (New York: Penguin Books U.S.A., Inc., 1957), p. 80.

18. Samuel Beckett, *Waiting for Godot* (New York: Grove Press/Atlantic, Inc., 1954), p. 61.

19. Walter de La Mare, "The Listeners" in *Collected Poems* (London: Faber and Faber, Ltd., 1942), pp. 284–285.

20. Lewis Carroll, *Alice's Adventures in Wonderland* in *The Annotated Alice* (New York: Clarkson N. Potter, Inc. Publisher, 1960), p. 134.

21. Alessandro Manzoni, *The Betrothed* (London: Penguin Books, 1972), p. 363. All quotations are from this edition. Reproduced by permission of Penguin Books Ltd.

22. Edgar Alan Poe, *The Fall of the House of Usher and Other Tales* (New York: The New American Library of World Literature, Inc., 1960), p. 98.

23. Emily Dickinson, *Final Harvest, Emily Dickinson's Poems,* selections and introduction by Thomas H. Johnson (Boston: Little, Brown, and Company, 1961), p. 25. This poem's number in the *Complete Poems of Emily Dickinson* is 214.

24. Nathaniel Hawthorne, *The Celestial Railroad and Other Stories* (New York: The New American Library, Inc., A Signet Classic, 1963), p. 115. All quotations are from this edition.

25. Charles Dickens, *Dombey and Son* (Part One) in *The Works of Charles Dickens,* vol. 14 (New York: Peter Fenelon Collier, Publisher, 1900), p. 138.

26. John Steinbeck, *The Grapes of Wrath* (New York: Penguin Books U.S.A., Inc., 1992), pp. 20–22, 60.

27. Seamus Heaney, "Crediting Poetry: The Nobel Lecture, 1995" in *Opened Ground: Selected Poems 1966–1996* (New York: Farrar, Straus, and Giroux, 1998), p. 422.

28. Leo Tolstoy, *Anna Karenin,* translated by Rosemary Edmonds (New York: Penguin Books, 1978), pp. 572 and 578.

29. Eudora Welty, "A Worn Path" in *A Curtain of Green and Other Stories* (San Diego, New York, London: Harcourt Brace Jovanovich, Publishers, An HBJ Modern Classic, 1991), p. 218. All quotations are from this edition.

30. Oscar Wilde, *The Picture of Dorian Gray* (New York, Modern Library Edition, 1985), p. 8. All quotations are from this edition.

31. Theodore Dreiser, *Sister Carrie* (New York: New American Library, A Signet Classic, 1961), p. 99. All quotations are from this edition.

32. Lewis Carroll, *Through the Looking Glass* in *The Annotated Alice* (New York: Clarkson N. Potter, Inc./Publisher, 1960), pp. 225–227.

33. Dorothy Parker, "Indian Summer" in *The Collected Poetry of Dorothy Parker* (New York: The Modern Library, Random House, 1936), p. 64.

34. L. Frank Baum, *The Wizard of Oz* (New York: The Bobbs-Merrill Company, 1944), p. 147.

35. Kenneth Grahame, "A White-washed Uncle" in *The Golden Age* (Berkeley, California: Ten Speed Press, 1993), pp. 4 and 29 ff.

36. Emily Dickinson, *Final Harvest, Emily Dickinson's Poems,* selections and introduction by Thomas H. Johnson (Boston: Little, Brown, and Company, 1961), p. 137. This poem's number in the *Complete Poems of Emily Dickinson* is 547.

37. Herman Melville, *Moby Dick* (New York: Random House edition, 1930), pp. 132–135. All quotations are from this edition.

38. Verses from *The New American Bible:* Proverbs 14:15; 15:17; 16:32; 16:24; 17:28; 25:19; 26:23; 26:17.

39. Dorothy Parker, "Unfortunate Coincidence" and "Comment" in *The Collected Poetry of Dorothy Parker* (New York: The Modern Library, Random House, 1936), pp. 40 and 43.

40. Samuel Beckett, *Waiting for Godot* (New York: Grove Press/Atlantic, Inc., 1954), pp. 10–11. All quotations are from this edition.

41. Charles Dickens, *Hard Times* (New York and London: Bantam Books, Inc., 1985), p. 201. All quotations are from this edition.

42. A. Philippa Pearce, *Tom's Midnight Garden* (New York: HarperCollins Publishers, Harper Trophy edition, 1992), p. 217. All quotations are from this edition.

43. Eudora Welty, "A Visit of Charity" in *A Curtain of Green and Other Stories* (San Diego, New York, London: Harcourt Brace Jovanovich, Publishers, An HBJ Modern Classic, 1991), p. 174. All quotations are from this edition.

44. John 12:31 ff. quotation taken from *The New American Bible* translation.

45. John Henry Newman, "Lead, Kindly Light" in *Great Poems of the English Language* (New York: Tudor Publishing Company, 1933), p. 644.

46. William Wordsworth, "Ode (Intimations of Immortality)" in *Wordsworth: Selected Poetry,* edited by Nicholas Roe (New York: Penguin Books U.S.A., 1992), p. 207.

47. Herman Melville, *Moby Dick* (New York: Random House edition, 1930), p. 177. All quotations are from this edition.

48. Isak Dinesen, "The Cardinal's Third Tale" in *Last Tales* (New York: Vintage Books, A Division of Random House, 1975), pp. 74–75. All quotations taken from this edition.

49. Evelyn Waugh, *Brideshead Revisted* (Boston: Little, Brown, and Company, 1945), p. 328. All quotations are from this edition.

50. Lewis Carroll, *Alice's Adventures in Wonderland* in *The Annotated Alice* (New York: Clarkson N. Potter, Inc./ Publisher, 1960), p. 37. All quotations are taken from this edition.

51. George Eliot, *Silas Marner* as contained in the *Works of George Eliot,* vol. 15 (New York: Peter Fenelon Collier, no date, probably ca. 1890), pp. 122, 124–125.

52. Evelyn Waugh, *Helena, A Novel* (Boston, Little, Brown, and Company, 1950), p. 47.

53. John McCrae, "In Flanders Fields" in *Great Poems of the English Language* (New York: Tudor Publishing Company, 1933), p. 1235.

54. Wilfred Owen, *The Collected Poems of Wilfred Owen* (New York: New Directions Books, 1964), p. 86.

About the Author

Geoff Wood holds a doctorate in theology and a licentiate in scripture from The Catholic University of America in Washington, D.C., and the Pontifical Biblical Institute in Rome. He is retired from an early academic career in religious studies and subsequent employment in the evaluation of human services at the national and local levels. Currently, he lives in Sonoma, California, where he continues to offer adult religious education courses at the parish and diocesan levels. He has been writing weekly essays for several Catholic parishes since 1989.

Acknowledgments continued from page iv.

Excerpt from *The Grapes of Wrath* by John Steinbeck, copyright 1939, renewed © 1967 by John Steinbeck. Used by permission of Viking Penguin, a division of Penguin Group (U.S.A.) Inc.

Excerpt from *Helena* reprinted by permission of s11/sterling Lord Literistic, Inc. Copyright by Evelyn, Esta Waugh.

Excerpt from *Last Tales* by Isak Dinesen, copyright © 1957 by Random House, Inc. Used by permission of Random House, Inc.

Excerpts from "Crediting Poetry" from *Opened Ground: Selected Poems 1966 –1996* by Seamus Heaney. Copyright © by Seamus Heaney. Reprinted by permission of Farrar, Straus, and Giroux, LLC.

Excerpts from *The Poems of Emily Dickinson* reprinted by permission of the publishers and the Trustees of Amherst College, Thomas H. Johnson, ed., Cambridge, Massachusetts: The Belknap Press of Harvard University Press, Copyright © 1951, 1955, 1979, 1983 by the President and Fellows of Harvard College.

Excerpts from "Comment," copyright 1926, © renewed 1954 by Dorothy Parker, "Indian Summer," copyright 1926, renewed © 1954 by Dorothy Parker, from *The Portable Dorothy Parker* by Dorothy Parker, edited by Brendan Gill. Used by permission of Viking Penguin, a division of Penguin Group (U.S.A.) Inc.

Excerpts from *Remembrance of Things Past: Volume 1* by Marcel Proust, translated by C. K. Scott Moncrieff and Terence Kilmartin, copyright © 1981 by Random House, Inc. and Chatto and Windus. Used by permission of Random House, Inc.

Excerpt from *Tom's Midnight Garden* by Philippa Pearce (OUP, 1998) copyright © Oxford University Press, 1958, reproduced by permission of Oxford University Press.